SPECIAL PEOPLE

To Samantha
Best wishes
Pam Young

Pam Young

Pamela Richards Publications

First published in 2009 by
Pamela Richards Publications,
4 Lancaster Way, Clifton, York, YO30 5ZA.

Printed and bound in Great Britain by
York Publishing Services,
Little Hallfield Lane, York

*The places, characters and events described in this
book are based on an amalgamation of places, people and events I have known or in which I have been
involved, and should not be taken as referring to
any specific individual or place, with two notable
exceptions: Sam has asked for his real name and
details to be used, and 'Peter' is a pseudonym for a
real person.*

ISBN 978-0-9558822-2-7

For my lovely husband, Richard, without whose love and support this book would not have been written; and for Hilary and Kath

Acknowledgements

I should like to thank:

Tiz Bacon and Beth Shurter for proof-reading the book and suggesting improvements with so much patience and tact;

Peter Bacon and Brian Sage for interpreting my ideas for the cover so brilliantly;

All the dedicated, professional, educational Staff with whom it has been my pleasure to work over the years, especially those who have encouraged me in the writing of this book;

The many other friends who have shown an interest and encouraged me;

The former pupils and their parents who I have been able to contact, and who have kindly given their consent for me to use their stories; and

All the other special children without whom the book would not have been written!

One Boy and His Dog!

It was not until I was forty three years old that I finally realised what I wanted to be when I grew up. Obviously a bit of a late developer, I had sympathy with children who had learning difficulties and so I decided that my teaching career should go in their direction. I had been a mainstream Primary School Teacher for twenty one years and had always enjoyed finding new ways to teach reading to the SEN (Special Educational Needs) children. I had given up my job when I married my second husband, Richard, in 1989, and since then I had done supply work; some long term, some short term. The novelty of that was wearing off, although there were advantages to it, the biggest one being that you didn't have to attend staff meetings!

I needed a game plan to achieve my goal so when I saw a flyer for a course for a Certificate in Advanced Educational Studies (Teaching SEN children Level 1) at our local college I signed up immediately. I obtained that in 1994, the Level 2 in 1995 and a Post-Graduate Diploma in 1996. The Certificate in Teaching Children with Dyslexia came the following year. You can tell that I was very serious about my new career!

Meanwhile my friend Marjorie, who had the job that I wanted - a School Based Additional Tuition Tutor, working with children who had Statements and so had SEN - had decided to move to another job. Aha! She only worked for four hours with two pupils but I wanted those hours! I rang up her boss, Vanessa, the person in charge of the Special Educational Needs

Service, to ask if I could be considered. She knew me anyway (and yet still considered me for the job!) as I had done the Dyslexia course run by her and her colleagues, and she knew about my intention to work with SEN children. The first time I rang she wasn't there, nor the second time, nor the third and so on. I kept leaving messages and waited for the 'phone call that would change my life.

After two weeks of constant badgering, Vanessa rang me, and agreed to consider me for the post. I'd probably worn her down with all my 'phone calls!

All the formalities involved in applying for a new job completed, I was asked to teach a seven year old boy who had AD/HD (Attention Deficiency/ Hyperactivity Disorder) - gulp! - at a local Infant School and an eleven year old girl with learning difficulties in the adjoining Junior School; a total of four hours per week. Well, it was a start.

As this was May and the girl would move on to her Secondary School in July I was not expected to work miracles with her - just as well, really - but the boy was seen as a more long term job. In fact Ben and I spent the next four years together, until he went off to Secondary School. Now, for your first job as an SBAT Tutor you really do not want a child with AD/HD, particularly this one. I had seen him reduce teachers to tears and cause havoc when I had been teaching on supply in the Infant School. But, with the enthusiasm of somebody in a new job, I set off on my first morning, full of high hopes and a fortifying breakfast.

I parked my car very carefully in St Luke's Primary School car park - schools never have car parks that are big enough, so a shoe horn is the first requirement for an SBAT Tutor. St Luke's was a building typical of the 1960s - all steel frame, concrete and glass, hell to heat in the winter and a greenhouse in the summer, with about as much charm as Alcatraz on a wet day! I eventually fought my way through the security system into the school where the lovely Secretary welcomed me as an old friend. Mary always had a warm smile for everyone and a kind word when things were not going well, which they often didn't. Conversely, she was the first to offer congratulations when things did go well.

When I told her who I had come to see, she went pale and gave me the kind of look she might have given an intended victim of the Spanish Inquisition.

"My, he's a ..."

"Challenge?" I queried, as she searched for the right word.

"Mm, yes, that will do, although it wasn't actually the word that I had in mind."

She smiled sympathetically at me and promised to give me a stiff Gin and Tonic - well, a cup of tea anyway - when I came back. (At least she didn't say if I came back!) Thoroughly unnerved by now I set off for the classroom, feeling like Daniel going into the lions' den.

I had rung Vanessa to let her know when I would be teaching Ben as she wanted to come and observe me to see if I was going to be suitable for the post. I collected Ben from his classroom and noted with some dismay the very relieved look on the teacher's face.

He was a plump child, with long fair hair desperately

in need of a good barber, and was dressed in what had once been a smart school uniform. However, as he was fond of fighting, by then it was in a state which would have caused most self-respecting tramps to turn their nose up at it!

The look on his face was one which said only too clearly that school was a total waste of time and that I was an annoying irrelevance. As you might guess, in terms of boosting my confidence in my new job, this introduction scored minus five.

Fortunately, the room we were to work in was just across the corridor; if it had been any further away I couldn't have kept up with him as he raced across the corridor like a rocket, flung open the door and raced around the room.

One of the characteristics of children with behavioural difficulties can be the ability to ignore you totally as if you had ceased to be. My exhortations to come and see what I had brought with me for him met with no response. Whatever I said, I had ceased to exist or I seemed to have lapsed into speaking Chinese. Ben hurtled around picking things up and flinging them wherever he pleased.

So, let's think this through then. Any time within the next half an hour my new boss will be coming to see whether I am a fit person to teach children with Special Needs. My whole new career would depend on what happened in the next few minutes. Right, emergency action was called for. My initial reaction was to panic but I managed to quash this (mostly by imagining my pay cheque - this had worked many times when I had been a Supply Teacher).

I had a bag of small toys I was planning to use as a

reward for good behaviour. I got this out, chose two and started to play with them on the carpet, seemingly ignoring Ben but keeping tabs on him out of the corner of my eye. It worked! Ben came over and demanded, "What are you doing?"

I explained that these toys were from my Reward bag which children who behaved well could choose from at the end of the lesson.

"Can I have a go?" was his next question.

I was ready with my answer.

"Yes, when you've been good. Come and sit down here."

I got up and indicated the desk.

"Then you can choose one to play with when we've talked to each other."

I held my breath and - oh yes - he sat down next to me at the desk.

All this time I was listening for the sound of the door opening and Vanessa walking in. I could feel my body tensing even more as I heard every sound in the corridor.

Still, at least he was sitting down now and he was listening to me, although eye contact had not been established. It is important to get children to look at you when they talk to you, but obviously I was going to have to take things slowly.

I had been given his reading book and when I saw it my heart sank! Talk about boring!

The red pig sat down.

The sad dog sat down.

The big cat sat down etc etc etc.

Ben looked at the book dismissively and tried to knock it off the desk.

"I'm not reading that!" he declared and turned his back on me. I felt like saying, no, you and me both, but the teacher had asked me to read some with him and I was trying hard to make a good impression. ("Creep!" I hear someone say!)

So, I started to read the page but I inserted Ben's name instead of the red pig. I saw his body stiffen so he was obviously listening. I carried on, making Ben the star of the story. I was soon aware that he had turned around.

"Does it really say that?" he said.

"No," I replied, "but we could write a story with you in it and then read it. Would you like that?"

He nodded reluctantly. "Huh, I suppose so," he said grudgingly. So that's what we did and by the time that Vanessa did walk through the door he was sitting quietly, illustrating our story. Alleluia!

Vanessa looked at the two of us and said to me, "He seems to be very calm."

"Yes," I said. "We've just written a short story, read it and now Ben is doing the picture." Meanwhile I was thinking to myself, thank goodness you didn't come at the beginning of the lesson when he was bouncing off the walls!

She looked at what we had done, at my lesson plans and targets, and tried to have a chat with Ben. She could recognise a lost cause though and I could recognise a child who was losing interest and would soon start playing up again.

"Well, Pam, I'm sure you'll be fine. I'll leave you to carry on," she said and went out of the door.

I heaved a huge sigh of relief and started to breathe normally again. Isn't it amazing how long you can hold your breath without realising?

Yes, oh yes - I was officially an SBAT Tutor - I had the job I'd wanted!

I came back down to earth as Ben, seeing that my mind was temporarily on other things, made a grab for my toy bag. This was going to be a challenging job but I was going to make it work!

Ben was very hard work for me but at least I was able to take him back to his class after forty minutes. Stella, his teacher, had him for the rest of the time and I did my best to support her in a difficult year for her.

She was a lovely lady, with the same expectations of behaviour as I had, and with our firm, consistent attitude to him we managed to survive. With similar outlooks and standards there was no way that Ben could play one off against the other, which he would have loved to have done.

One day I walked into the classroom and looked for Ben in vain. Oh yes, perhaps he was absent! (I know I shouldn't have thought that, but he was going through a difficult period and I was wishing that for Stella too!)

I raised my eyebrows at Stella. I didn't want to interrupt the lesson as she was in full flow.

"Ah, Mrs Young," she greeted me. "I'm afraid that Ben is with the Head." Mr Sowersby was the Headteacher, a strict disciplinarian but a very nice man. He was very tall and had a small goatee beard that was streaked with flashes of grey, unlike his full head of jet black hair.

"Oh," I looked at her quizzically. "Is there a problem?"

The children were all agog as they waited to hear the gory details of Ben's latest exploits all over again. It's amazing how inquisitive most children can be, especially if they think that blood will be shed, in a metaphorical sense!

When I was a Classroom Teacher and things were getting a bit noisy, all I had to do was call out a child's name and say, "What _are_ you doing?" and instantly there would be silence.

Stella sighed and shook her head.

I took the hint and said, "I'll go down to Mr Sowersby's office, shall I?"

She nodded and sighed again.

I tiptoed out of the classroom and walked down the corridor. What on earth had he done this time? I was quite used to hearing about Ben's exploits but the look on Stella's face had told me that this time it was rather serious.

The Secretary would have filled me in but she was busy seeing to parents so she mouthed at me to knock on the Head's door.

The resulting, "Come in!" sounded weary and it was only half-past nine!

I put my head round the door to see a cross-looking Headteacher, drumming his fingers on his desk, and Ben sitting on a chair in the corner, looking very shame-faced.

"Ah, Mrs Young." His face brightened as he realised that I would take Ben off his hands.

"I understand that there has been a problem, Mr Sowersby, but I'm afraid I don't know what has happened."

At the same time I caught a whiff of something that

was certainly not fragrance of the week in the Avon catalogue.

Mr Sowersby winced, as the thought of telling me the story would bring the whole episode back to mind again.

"Well, perhaps Ben would like to tell you what happened this morning."

Ben looked as if this was the last thing that he wanted to do. He looked thunderously at me as only he could do.

Then he looked at Mr Sowersby's face and realised that he meant business. He cast his eyes down to the carpet and mumbled something unintelligible.

"We couldn't hear that, Ben, speak up!"

Again he looked thunderously at me and then he blurted out, "Scruffy came to school."

Ah, the picture was becoming clearer. Everyone knew that Ben's Mum had a Pit Bull Terrier which frightened the living daylights out of anybody who was unfortunate enough to get within two miles of it. (This was in the days before it became illegal to own one.) As a single Mum we assumed that she had it for protection, though if you had seen the tattoos on her, it would have been a brave man who would have tangled with that particular lady.

Bit by bit, the story began to emerge. Ben regularly came to school on his own, having got himself some breakfast as Mum was too idle to get out of bed.

That morning Scruffy had managed to get out of the garden as Ben hadn't shut the gate properly. He knew the gate had to be kept bolted, but his best mate was passing by at the vitally important moment when he should have fastened the catch properly, instead of admiring the latest football stickers.

Scruffy had followed Ben all the way to school as parents and children had all been throwing them selves behind hedges and into gardens to get away from the vicious dog.

The children who were already in the playground had hysterics as the dog lumbered up to them, licking its chops, with a look that said, "Oh good, breakfast!"

Mothers and fathers had reacted quite reasonably by panicking and hurling themselves at the locked school doors, demanding to be let in.

Unfortunately, by the time the Staff had realised what was going on and had opened the doors, Scruffy had caused pandemonium and had managed to leave his calling card as well. Ben, in his attempts to catch the dog, had skidded in the aforementioned calling card, slipped and got most of it on his trousers. Ah, the whiff of something rather unpleasant was now explained!

Ben had been given clean clothes to change into but some smells do linger.

By now somebody had called the Police on their mobile 'phone and soon the sound of approaching sirens was added to the general mayhem. As the School Secretary frantically dialled Ben's Mum's house she was not relishing the idea of being shouted at by a woman with tattoos who is determined to get her beauty sleep. Boy, was she cross! Even more so when she realised that she would have to get out of bed, get dressed and come down to school.

Eventually she appeared, mouthing off at anybody and everybody who got in her way. She caught the dog, which by this time was going berserk in an empty playground as parents had either got their children into school or had taken them home. Her language was a little choice, to say the very least, especially when she was apprehended by a rather large burly policeman and asked to account for the dog's appearance at school.

She had then torn into Ben, telling him exactly what she thought of him, and what she would do to him when he got home.

By this time, Ben was out of control - remember that he had AD/HD - so he swore at the Headteacher, never a wise course of action. Ben was not in any fit state to be with the rest of the class, and so Mr Sowersby had taken it upon himself to calm him down, and try to get him ready for me to teach him. Sometimes, though, you know when to admit defeat and as I walked Ben down to our room, I knew that I would have to abandon any work I had planned.

He lagged behind me all the way down the corridor and dragged his heels as he slumped down into his chair.

I was hoping that inspiration would come to me and that I would find the right words to cope with this situation.

But then I realised that words were not necessary at that moment as this boy, who could be belligerent, foul-mouthed, defiant and impossible, burst into tears and sobbed. His body shook as he put his head on his arms on the desk and gave in to the misery he was feeling. If I had a mother like that who had threatened me with goodness knows what, I would have cried as well.

I longed to put my arms around him to comfort him

but as I was alone with him I just daren't. Yes, I know that sounds wimpish but you couldn't be too careful when on your own with a child. Instead, I put my hand on his arm and told him that it was alright to cry, and then I sat there until he stopped and got himself back together again.

The whole of my forty minute lesson was spent in trying to get him on an even keel so that I could take him back to the classroom. When I thought about it, he hadn't been malicious. He just hadn't fastened a gate properly.

§

Gradually, bit by bit, we all saw an improvement in Ben, and eventually he would walk to the room we were to work in, and actually sit down and do some work.

The day came when we decided to let him walk back to the classroom on his own. He had been asking if he could do that for some time but there were so many distractions we weren't sure he would arrive at the classroom door before school finished for the day, if at all. Technically he was in my care until he got back to the classroom, so I would be the one who would carry the can if he decided to go AWOL or get up to mischief.

I explained to him that we were going to allow him to walk back to the classroom on his own and his eyes lit up. Was that through pleasure at being given this privilege or was he planning what he could do with his freedom? I really didn't feel very confident about this so, as Ben set off from the room, I followed at a very discreet distance, hiding behind cupboards and cloakrooms so that he wouldn't see me.

Unfortunately, the Headteacher could see **me**, but not Ben, so he had no idea what I was doing. You know sometimes you just feel that someone is watching you though you can't see them? I spun round to see him gazing at me with a puzzled expression on his face. Of course, when I stopped to explain what I was doing I lost sight of Ben, but, bless him, he had gone straight back to his class and hadn't put a foot wrong.

§

That reminds me of the time many years before when I had been a Classroom Teacher teaching six and seven year olds. We were doing a project on the environment and litter, and that day we were going to be Wombles and pick up all the litter in the school grounds. We would then analyse it and do various activities based on the curriculum.

Disaster struck this particular morning, when I came into school early and realised that another class had done exactly the same thing yesterday. There was not one piece of rubbish anywhere in the playgrounds! I had promised the children that we would do this and they were looking forward to it so I didn't want to disappoint them.

I thought hard. I looked around the classroom for a bit of rubbish, and went out into the playground to search the bins. Good, there was some litter in there and with what I had found already I should be alright.

I started to fling this litter all over the playground, never thinking how peculiar it must look to anyone else. As before, I suddenly felt that I was being watched and turned round to find the Headteacher and the Caretaker looking out of the window at my antics with looks of bewilderment on their faces. That took a bit of explaining, I can tell you!

2

Perils and Pleasures

So, what does a School Based Additional Tuition (SBAT) Tutor do? The Tutor is a teacher, with much experience in the classroom, who has specialised in teaching children with Special Educational Needs (SEN).

Children with severe/moderate learning difficulties, or other problems, were given a Statement, a legal document which stated what their needs were and the help that they should receive. If the child was to be educated in a mainstream school this often included extra teaching by an SBAT Tutor in Literacy and/or Numeracy.

The maximum time awarded was two and a half hours a week but it could vary from an hour to the maximum. Extra help was usually given in the classroom by a Pupil Support Assistant (PSA) who would liaise closely with the SBAT Tutor. Well, she would when they were both free at the same time. This was usually done at break times, lunch times or even over the 'phone on an evening, in an extreme situation.

The Tutor also had to liaise with the Class Teacher, parents and the Special Needs Co-ordinator (SENCo) and this was one of the most difficult aspects of the job. I once had a discussion with a SENCo in the toilets, killing two birds with one stone, so to speak! The child was almost always taken out of the class and worked either in a one-to-one situation with the Tutor, with one other child, or in a small group. Obviously, the more children who could be given extra help, the happier the teachers were, but the other children had to be at a similar stage of their learning as the child who had the Statement.

This could lead to all sorts of problems. If the second child was from a younger year group, the child with a Statement, who often had little self-esteem, could feel even less confident, particularly if the other child always did better than him or her. This balance was often difficult to achieve and more than once I had to be quite assertive, as the welfare of the child with the Statement was of paramount importance to me. At other times the choice of another child to work with was inspired and worked perfectly.

The children had to get on well and often it was a good idea for a child with behaviour problems to be paired with a child who was a good role model.

As you can see, the job was fraught with difficulties before you even started!

When I was a Class Teacher I would arrive at school at eight o'clock and nab one of the parking spaces without any difficulty. Schools never have big enough car parks and as a peripatetic teacher, turning up at any time of the day, I always worried that there would be absolutely nowhere to park.

Parking in a residential street quite a way from the school was the last resort but with heavy bags to carry and usually only two minutes to get into the school, sign in, find a room, set the work up and then collect the child, this was not my preferred option.

I think I'm a reasonable driver but parking has never been my strong point, and as I spotted a space in the car park which my husband could park a double-decker bus in, I wished I had his confidence and skills. I would rarely risk it. The thought of having to go and find the Headteacher to tell them that I had bumped his or her precious car was too awful to contemplate!

Nowadays, as more children with SEN are being included in mainstream schools, with the inevitable involvement of more professional Staff visiting the child, there are more comings and goings in car parks, so I would hope to find a space recently vacated by one of my colleagues.

Leaving the school proved to be as problematic as arriving! I once came back to my car and, having only five minutes to get to a school that was fifteen minutes away, I was, understandably, in a rush, so I stared in disbelief at the lorry that was completely blocking the entrance to the car park!

Oh, calamity! I thought. (Or something like that.)

I searched the outside of the school looking for the likely culprits and when I found them was amazed to hear them say, "But this is a school so we thought that you'd be here all day!"

"Yeah, right, but some of us are peripatetic staff," I yelled over my shoulder as I sprinted towards my car and then sat waiting while the driver ambled over and slowly got into his cab. Aaaargh!

So, having parked, I would then try to enter the school. As everybody knows, while in the old days one just walked in, this isn't possible nowadays. Each school had a four-digit code which could be tapped into a key pad and hey presto! The door would open as long as I had put the right numbers in. Well, my excuse was that with maybe four schools to visit, remembering these codes, plus the code for my burglar alarm at home, various PINs for the bank etc, was rather challenging.

The schools would, rightly, change their codes from time to time, and would sometimes forget to tell me, so even if I correctly remembered a code it could be the wrong one!

Sometimes I would just have to disturb the Secretary, or any passing adult, and parry their comment of, "Don't you know the code, Pam?" with a, "Sorry - yes, but I've forgotten it!" as I dashed past them in my usual haste.

In this job you were always clock-watching and, for me, one of the joys of retirement is not being so regulated by time.

As each Statemented child had different needs my resources were tailored to each one. Every child had a separate bag which I lugged out of my car boot into school and then had to lug around, looking for somewhere to work. This could be a huge problem and it will be a recurring one in this book. Well, I had to work somewhere and as many of my pupils had concentration or behaviour problems, a room with four walls and a door was my heart's desire.

Many a time, though, I found myself in a corridor trying to settle a child while what seemed like half the world walked by. Adults would appreciate the difficulty and would try to tiptoe past, but passing children would stop for a chat or would just call out, "Hi, Miss Young!" (The children often referred to me as Miss Young and although I always corrected them, it was a hopeless cause. Both names appear in this book, depending on who is talking to me!)

It was good they were friendly but in that situation I would have settled for being ignored.

Some schools put me in the staff room, which wasn't

ideal, and a few times I dragged a table and chairs into one of the larger stock cupboards, trying to ignore any feelings of claustrophobia and the inevitable lack of fresh air.

One new school had a lovely glass atrium in the middle of the building. Most of the people in the school used it as a passageway so it had its drawbacks, but I soon learned that this was nothing, as I would fry in Summer and shiver in the Winter.

Two Headteachers actually made me rooms, which had been large cupboards, which were used by other people when I wasn't there. I shall always be grateful to them. You know who you are!

An Educational Psychologist once told me that one of the best qualifications for the job was a strong back. It was a pity that I didn't have one then! A trampolining accident when I was in my mid-thirties (sounds good, doesn't it, but I was doing a taster session. My GP said I would have been better off taking up knitting!) had meant that I always had a weakness there. Getting my bags, which seemed to get heavier and heavier, into and out of a school wasn't easy. If I had more than one Statemented pupil in a school (which was often the case) then I had more bags, so the problem was exacerbated. You just had to manage so you did! I certainly wasn't the only one who struggled.

Having got my bags into school, found a suitable room and set the work and activities out, I then had to go and collect the child(ren). Sounds easy, doesn't it?

Usually I knocked on the classroom door and asked for whoever I needed and often the teacher and the child regarded me as the cavalry. I knocked on one door once and as the teacher turned to me it seemed that the whole class looked at me with pleading eyes, begging me to take them out as well. They were having a very fraught lesson! Some even put their hands together in mock prayer but put them down again very quickly as the teacher turned back to them. I think most of the children I took were pleased to see me, and the other children knew that they did work which was at their level, they played games as part of the lesson, and they came back with a sticker on their jumper. How good was that! I often had children asking if they could come to me, thinking that they would get an easy ride. This was not a reflection on the teachers, but on what one child vividly described as the 'stinki nashunal curicyoulum'!

Sometimes I would appreciate that I had arrived at the precise moment when the child was actually enjoying an activity, especially when it was some-thing out of the ordinary, like a visitor. I would try to encourage the teachers to tell me when this would be occurring but, as they had so much on their minds, this often didn't happen. It did sometimes, and then I would try to swap children's times around, but this only worked if I had more than one child in the school.

I once went into a classroom to find all the children poring over Ordnance Survey maps - yes, really! They were obviously fascinated, inspired by a good teacher, and as Tom, my pupil, looked up and saw that I had come for him, his face fell.

"Oh, Miss Young, this is really interesting! Couldn't I come later?"

Then, as he was a polite child, he said quickly, "It's not that I don't want to come; I just don't want to come at this minute!"

His teacher smiled and indicated that it would be fine for me to come back later for him. I was always prepared to accommodate the children if I could. What would have been the point of dragging Tom away from something he was enjoying?

Too often I had to take a child out of a lesson he wanted to be in - I found it very difficult when the class had swapped PE times with another class - and then I had to struggle to overcome their resentment.

When sorting out my timetable at the start of a term I always tried to avoid their PE, Music and Art lessons as many of my pupils were good at these subjects. Imagine being taken out of the one lesson you were good at and enjoyed!

However, trying to accommodate their likes and dislikes, and the Literacy and Numeracy lessons in each class and then in each school was a nightmare! I always heaved a huge sigh of relief when I managed to sort out my timetable.

Quite often I would go cheerfully down the corridor to the classroom only to find that the room was entirely empty! I would search the school, looking in all the places I could think of, like the computer suite, the hall, the playground, and if these drew a blank I would resort to the School Secretaries. They usually knew what was going on!

Of course the worst case scenario was when the class had gone out on a trip and the teacher had forgotten to tell me! If I had other pupils in the same school I could give them an extra lesson but at one school, which shall be nameless, I only had the one child and one Summer term the class went out on three trips and nobody informed me! I was quite philosophical about the first two occasions but felt really hacked off by the third time!

I started to look shamelessly on teachers' desks for letters that were being given out to the children, because a letter always had to go out to the parents every time a trip was arranged. The children themselves were often a good source of information!

The notice board on every staff room wall was also very useful for that, so I became used to keeping my ears and eyes open.

(I must admit that if a child with bad behaviour problems happened to be away or on a trip I heaved an almighty sigh of relief!)

Christmas was the worst time for all this. The class would often be having a party, watching the younger children in their Nativity Play, at a Carol Concert, out entertaining the Senior Citizens at the local Old Folks' Home or something similar.

A teacher once looked at my exasperated expression as I realised that my pupil would not be getting their lesson, and declared, "Oh Pam, why don't you relax, accept it, and come and watch the play with us? It is Christmas, you know!"

I smiled and gave in. That year I watched two Carol Concerts and four Nativity Plays!

Although I have dwelt on the difficulties in this job there were many advantages and it was the best job I ever had. For a start I didn't have to go to staff meetings, though I often chose to go to early morning diary meetings where the next week's activities were announced. If I did that I would have a much better idea of what was going on and where my pupils would be.

I didn't have to go out into the playground on duty, a job which I disliked intensely, especially when it was freezing cold! Trying to sort out disagreements and fights, or deciding whether a child was really hurt was not my idea of fun. (The rule of thumb was, the quieter a child was, the more serious it was. If a child screamed blue murder I was not too worried but a pale, soundless child sent alarm bells ringing.)

I was my own boss, and working outside of the confines of the National Curriculum, I could teach the children what they really needed to know, at their own level.

I could go off at a tangent if something interesting came up, and frequently had to abandon my planned work completely as I worked round the child's needs. I loved trying to find different ways of teaching the same concept and trying to make it fun for the child and for myself. I used my imagination to devise various games and then spent hours customising them and making them look attractive.

I had to be very flexible and face any situation with a calmness which I didn't always feel inside, and I had to use my abilities to face problems and act accordingly. A sense of humour and a big smile often helped!

The humour could also come from the children, although I must admit that it was rare for my children to be able to laugh at themselves. One day I was met by the Headteacher of a school where I was teaching some Travellers' children.

"I'm glad you've come," she declared. "Billy and Eli are in our production of Joseph and his Amazing Technicolour Dreamcoat. They're really keen and have been coming to all the rehearsals but there's a song in French and they just can't get the hang of it. Could you go over the words with them for me, please?"

I thought I would rather perform brain surgery really as I wasn't too optimistic about my chances of success, but game for anything, I set off to get the boys with the script in my hand.

"What are we doing today?" enquired Eli, looking at the rather large sheaf of papers with some suspicion. I duly explained.

Billy's eyes twinkled. "Eh, Miss Young, we're not right good at speaking English, are we, never mind French?"

We laughed together, and though we all had a good stab at it, we decided that maybe they should just mime the words!

When I went to see them in the performance one evening and that particular song started, I couldn't help grinning at the boys and they both grinned back, while confidently mouthing silently!

That was another perk of the job. Having arranged so many Nativity and other plays, I could now attend performances of all my pupils and know that I wasn't responsible for a single thing. I didn't have any of the stress, although I could sometimes feel very nervous as the time came for their big moment. I think I was usually more nervous than they were!

I'm sure there were many highlights but I think the funniest one was seeing one of my big butch eleven year olds dressed up in a pink tutu as a ballerina! That boy had some courage!

I once had to deliver something to a Pupil Referral Unit which catered for older pupils with behaviour problems. There were some very difficult children and I really respected the Staff who worked there. It was a job that I couldn't have done.

Anyway, this particular day they were fund-raising for Children in Need, as most of the schools were that day. The Secretary who took the envelope from me was in fancy dress and, as she explained to me what they were doing, she asked, "Have you seen Aaron yet?"

Now believe me, Aaron was a tough guy and I wouldn't normally stick around if I saw him coming! My face must have said it all because she grinned at me and said, "No, you really must see him. He's in drag and he looks fantastic!"

My mind boggled and just at that moment Aaron swaggered into my view in all his glory. He had on a blonde wig, full make up, which with an incipient moustache looked really surreal, a purple and pink lurex sparkly dress and three inch high heels.

He grinned at me and, doing a twirl, said, "What do you reckon?"

I was a bit dumbstruck to say anything at first then I blurted out, "Did you walk to school like that?"

"Yep!" he declared. "No problem!"

The Secretary leaned over to me and said in a loud voice, "Aaron's being sponsored to do this. Somebody bet him he wouldn't dare do it and he's already made a lot of money for Children in Need."

They both looked pointedly at me. I could take a hint

and anyway I might meet Aaron again!

I opened my purse and was rather taken aback to see that I didn't have any £1 coins. It was costing me a fortune that day, going round different schools and participating in all the activities, but I so admired Aaron's bravery and the way he was putting up with all the ribald jokes and comments that I dug deep and came up with a £5 note. I was happy to contribute to his sponsorship money. Mind you, the Staff weren't daft - it was the Secretary who collected the money for him!

I enjoyed working on my own but at times it could be a bit lonely. When the attack on a school in Dunblane happened and the news started to come through on the radio, I was sitting in my car in a lay-by, eating my lunch en route to another school. It was a school I had only just started to work in and as yet I didn't know many of the Staff. The news was so horrific that I desperately wanted to talk to somebody about it and share my feelings, but at that particular moment I was isolated and alone. By the time I got to the school the lunch time break was over and I had to wait until I got home before I could talk to my husband about the full horror of it.

We had training days at the beginning of every term, run by the Inclusion Support Service, as it became known, for whom I worked. It was a chance for us to spend time with our colleagues and catch up on news, as we were usually just ships that passed in the night by the very nature of our jobs.

They were a lovely lot of people, colleagues and bosses alike, and I admired their professionalism, dedication, and commitment. Fortunately we all had a similar sense of humour and the room rang with shared laughter and cheerful chatter. Vanessa, the Head of the Service, often had great difficulty in bringing us to order!

The training meant that we were up to date in all aspects of SEN initiatives, but also in what was going on in the National Curriculum. My head would be buzzing after one of these days and I would often feel overwhelmed by the enormity and responsibility of the job.

All I could do was my best to try to educate my pupils and give them a good experience of school. If they were happy and learning at the same time, so much the better. When I was having one of my less confident, bleaker moments, then I consoled myself with the thought that, in the case of a child with behaviour problems, at least I was giving the teacher and the class a break!

3

It's An 'Eggciting' Life!

The young boy sat down at the other side of the table and stared at the floor. He was very slight in build, short for his age and he had a look of misery etched all over his face. He wore round, black glasses which gave him an owlish look.

"I hate school," he said at last. "It's boring!"

He glanced up at me, as if sizing me up, then returned his gaze to the floor in despair. What he really meant was that he hated school because he couldn't read, spell, write, or do number work, and his self-esteem was at rock bottom.

I tried to engage him in conversation about himself, his family, anything. His air of dejection was quite infectious and I was quite relieved to take him back to his classroom.

Sam, as he was called, had a Statement because of his Special Needs, and I had been called in to teach him basic Literacy skills for two and a half hours a week. He attended Milderton Primary School, a modern single storey school in a pleasant, leafy suburb.

Milderton was one of the larger Primary Schools in the city, with a catchment area that covered a wide diversity of property, both council and private. Built in the 1980s, it had many additional rooms 'tacked on' and was such a rabbit warren of a place that, given my sense of direction is poor at any time, I needed a map to find my way around it! Fortunately, the Secretary was able to provide me with one, but as soon as I had collected the pupils it proved unnecessary, for even though they had Special Needs, they had no problems in navigating the maze of corridors! (I also had problems with all kinds of modern technology, such as digital cameras, video recorders etc, and the children, even ones with severe difficulties, were again always able to help me out.)

I had been told that teaching Sam wouldn't be an easy task, but I could see that for myself. However, if Sam was downhearted and feeling miserable, I certainly wasn't. I took Book One of the reading scheme we were to tackle home with me and looked at the vocabulary. The words 'egg' and 'black box' appeared early on in the book and I decided that I could easily make some visual aids for these words. So, I made a little black box out of cardboard and I boiled an egg. I wrote the appropriate words on them and next day collected Sam from his classroom with high hopes. He didn't look any less miserable, and he came out to me with an 'I'll just have to tolerate her' look on his face.

I sat him down, took the egg from my bag, and said, "Here, Sam, catch!" Of course, he didn't know that the egg was hard boiled and, to give him his due, he stuck out his hands and managed to catch it. A slight look of interest came over his face.

"Throw it back!" I demanded, and thankfully caught it myself. His eyes opened even more widely when I threw it back to him and then, again, caught it myself when he threw it back at me. The third time I threw it to him, a look of horror came over his face as the egg slipped from between his fingers and fell to the floor.

His relief when he saw the crack on the egg, and realised that it was hard boiled, produced a smile.

"Cor, Miss, that gave me a shock!" and he grinned at me, although only fleetingly.

I picked the egg up and pointed out the word on the shell. I then wrote 'crack' on it, which was another word to be learnt. The black box was duly examined by Sam and he grudgingly admired my handiwork.

By the end of our session, we had begun to learn to read four new words, but more importantly, Sam was becoming interested and there was a tiny spark of enthusiasm there.

As we walked back to his classroom, and he passed other pupils, he told them all, "She throwed a egg at me, you know!" He seemed to be quite pleased and amused, but I could just see the headlines in the Sunday papers, '**Teacher throws egg at pupil!**'

I went straight to the Headteacher, Mr Fox, and rather sheepishly explained what I had done. He roared with laughter and then congratulated me for having found a way (albeit somewhat unorthodox) of getting through to Sam. As the Head of Milderton Primary School he was a bit unorthodox himself, but would fight tooth and nail to get the best for the children in his care. I learnt from him that rules and regulations were there to be broken if a child would benefit.

I taught Sam for four years and I enjoyed my time with him immensely. I had a really good relationship with him, and his family, who were always very supportive and appreciated everything we did. Would that this were always the case!

Sam loved to talk and although he was a serious little boy he was very gregarious and had lots of friends. I sometimes taught him how to cook and I would take him shopping for the ingredients, after we had chosen a recipe. I would usually take another child with us. Nearly everybody we passed had a cheery greeting for Sam, and the other boy and I often had to wait patiently as Sam had a long conversation with the lady on the checkout.

We decided to cook a meal for Sam's parents and his friend, Andrew, to demonstrate his new-found skills. The menu, chosen by Sam, consisted of Spaghetti Bolognaise followed by Black Forest gateau. The date was duly fixed, ingredients bought and parents and Andrew invited.

I was working in my room on that day just before going to get Sam to prepare everything. The School Secretary knocked on my door and came in looking a bit grim.

"It's Sam's parents. They've just rung up to say they can't come for lunch."

I looked aghast.

"But why ever not? Sam is so looking forward to them coming. This had better be good!"

"Well, I think when you hear, you'll understand. Sam's Dad is in bed with bronchitis and his Mum has just had some really bad news about her sister. She's just too upset to go anywhere."

I stared open-mouthed.

"Yes, I see what you mean!"

"Will you tell Sam, or will I?"

"No, I'll do it. I was just going to get him. Thanks for offering anyway."

I sat and thought for a while and then made my way down to Sam's classroom. There was no way we were going to abandon the meal after all our planning. He had been looking forward to it so much. I looked round the classroom door and beckoned to Sam. He had been looking out for me since nine o'clock so he shot out of his chair and set off eagerly down the corridor.

I waited until we got to the kitchen then I said, "Sam, there's something I want to talk to you about."

He looked at me with that resigned look I had seen so many times before.

"They're not coming are they?"

"No," I said as gently as I could. "Your Dad isn't well and your Mum is a bit upset about some news that she's had."

"I know, Miss Young. You don't have to worry about telling me."

"Oh right, Sam. I didn't know if you knew."

"Yeah, I heard them talking last night. Are we doing the meal then?"

I smiled at him.

"We certainly are, Sam. We can still do it for Andrew and I think that a few other people might pop in to see what a brilliant cook you are!"

We started to cook although we both felt rather subdued. At break time that morning I told as many of the Staff as possible that our star guests were unable to come.

"There's a huge Black Forest gateau to eat, so if anybody would like to sample it you would be most welcome."

If you mention food in any staff room you will immediately have everybody's attention.

"What time would this be?" asked Bob, one of the teachers, already licking his lips.

I knew that they wouldn't let us down. As Sam, Andrew and I ate our dessert, my hard-worked, busy colleagues all came to see us, tried the gateau and praised Sam's cooking to the hilt. Of course, nothing made up for his parents not being there, but the Staff came up trumps and made Sam's day.

The next time that we cooked we made all the food for my Year Six Leavers' party - twenty four sausage rolls, three pizzas, twelve buns, twelve flapjacks and a cake! Sam could beat a sponge mix to within an inch of its life so I had to keep my wits about me but his enjoyment and resulting pride made up for my exhaustion and stress!

Sam and I spent a lot of time talking and his oral skills were first rate. He had a very grown-up attitude to life and could discuss topics in a mature way that belied his tender years.

He told me one day that his Grandma had cancer and that she was very ill. In our daily sessions he told me how she was and it soon became apparent that Sam's parents were keeping nothing from him and that he was aware that she was not going to get better. I knew every last detail of that lady's illness and soon we were all aware that she didn't have long to live.

To get to Sam's classroom I had to walk down a long corridor that had lots of classrooms off it. As I walked into school that morning, first the Office Staff told me that Sam's Grandma had died, then almost all the classroom doors opened one after another and each teacher popped her head out and told me the same news. I wasn't due to see Sam until later that morning as I had other pupils to teach, so I crept into his classroom and whispered to him that he could come and see me in my room at break time if he wanted. He nodded briefly, then turned back to his work, his face impassive. I wondered if he would come instead of being with his friends at playtime.

I didn't go to the staff room at break time but sat in my room working. Very soon there was a knock on the door and Sam peeped in. I felt very honoured that he had chosen to come but I felt even more privileged as I listened to that young man tell me exactly how his Grandma had died (he had been at the bedside).

"It's for the best, you know," he said seriously. "She was in a lot of pain and now she's not. She really was suffering but not any more. Of course my Dad is upset and so am I but it will get better. I loved her and I've got some nice things to remember about her, but she had to go."

His sensible and accepting attitude impressed me greatly and not once did he give in to the tears which must have been lurking. Eventually he finished talking and told me that he would go out to play.

As soon as he had gone I wept. I wept for the family, for Sam and in gratitude for the close relationship that we had.

After a while I went to the staff room for a drink and as soon as the teachers saw me they offered **me** sympathy. I was reduced to a jelly by this brave little boy, but a very privileged jelly!

My favourite story about Sam was when I was going through the letters of the alphabet with him, saying the sounds that they make eg buh instead of bee for 'b'. I showed him the letter 'u', expecting the answer "uh". He stared hard at it in a lesson in concentration. You could never fault Sam for effort! After a while I said, "Shall I give you a clue, Sam?"

"No, no, I'll get it!" he assured me but after a few more minutes had elapsed he finally gave in.

"Go on then, I'll have a clue, please," he said.

"OK, this sound is at the beginning of something that you put up when it rains."

"Yes!" he shouted gleefully, "I've got it! Uh for 'ood!"

I couldn't bring myself to tell him that I was thinking of an umbrella, so at that particular school it was always uh for 'ood!

As Sam and I worked together we would chat away about anything and everything. We even watched the same television programmes sometimes which was a rarity. The choice of my pupils' viewing was seldom the same as mine!

One day we were chatting about food and about the *Two Fat Ladies* cookery programme that we had both watched the night before.

Sam regaled me with what one lady had said.

"Which one was it?" I questioned him.

"I don't know, but eh, Miss Young, she were a big lass!"

"Well, they're both pretty big, Sam!" I laughed.

"Yeah, but this one were really, really big!"

He was so skinny and slight himself that I suppose to him most people were on the large side.

Our talk turned to our respective lunches.

"What 'ave you got in your sandwich today, Miss Young?"

"My favourite, Sam, egg."

"Ooh, I love egg sandwiches. They're **my** favourite!"

"Yes, I'm really looking forward to lunch time. I'm

feeling very hungry today."

I felt very hungry every day but that was beside the point.

"What are you doing for your lunch?" I enquired.

"I'm staying for school dinners today," he said, in a voice totally devoid of enthusiasm. I looked closely at him.

"You don't sound very keen."

"I'm not. I don't like their dinners. I love egg sandwiches, though. They sound really nice."

He looked me in the eye. "You're lucky, aren't you, looking forward to egg sandwiches!"

I laughed. "Oh alright, Sam, I give in. Pass me my lunchbox from the cupboard over there."

He leapt up eagerly and, quick as a flash, the box was on the desk.

I got the sandwich out and did a quick Maths lesson on fractions for him as I divided it in half. Well, I tried never to miss an opportunity!

Sam's eyes were nearly popping out of his head with anticipation and he wolfed down every crumb with alarming speed.

He then looked at the small portion of sandwich that I had yet to finish.

"Not a chance, Sam, don't even think about it!"

He smiled. "No, I right enjoyed that, but I wouldn't eat any more of your lunch!"

Every day after that we had the same conversation and if I had egg sandwiches I always made an extra one. Even today, I can't eat an egg sandwich without thinking of Sam!

I still have the piece of writing that Sam did one day about his best friend.

It's An 'Eggciting' Life!

He wrote:

My best friend

My best friend is Mrs Young

because she helps me.

We both like egg

sandwiches

Most of my SEN pupils were good at something, whether it was Sport, Art, Music, Dancing or something else. Sam was no exception. He was brilliant at singing and playing the drums.

One day, when I went to pick him up from his classroom, I could see that he was bubbling over with excitement, and that he was desperate to tell me something.

"Guess what, Miss Young?"

He skipped happily along beside me, bursting with enthusiasm.

"Er, you've won the Lottery?" I questioned.

"No, I'm not old enough to do it, am I?" He gave me a 'Don't be silly, Miss Young' look.

"The Queen's asked you to go for tea at Buckingham Palace?"

Another disparaging look shot my way.

"Go on, then, you'd better tell me," I said, putting him out of his misery.

"Well, Mr Fox says I can play the drums at the end of term concert, and he says I can be the lead singer in a song six of us are doing. Isn't that brilliant?"

I smiled down at him.

"Yes, Sam, that is extremely brilliant and I can't wait to see the concert."

"But will you be able to come?" Sam was aware that I flitted from one school to another and that I had commitments elsewhere.

"Sam, whatever I am doing, wherever I am, I shall make the necessary arrangements and I will be there."

He beamed happily at me and I wondered just what I would have to do to keep my promise, although I would definitely keep it.

I was really pleased that Mr Fox had entrusted Sam with these tasks as I knew that he prided himself on the excellence of his concerts, and the children would spend a lot of time rehearsing and getting things just right.

Sure enough, in the next few weeks there would be times when I would go to collect Sam, only to be told that he was rehearsing with Mr Fox. I never minded as I knew that it was so important to Sam, and I could always swap his time with another child in the school so that he never lost out.

The day of the concert came very quickly. Just as well, really, as I don't think that Sam could contain his excitement any more. At last, here was something that he could excel at in front of the whole school and the parents. He was well aware that he was never going to be able to keep up with his classmates in academic subjects, but when it came to music - hey, he was top of the pops!

As we all filed into the school hall for the long-awaited performance the tension and excitement filled the air. Doting parents craned their necks to catch a glimpse of their little prodigies, while the teachers, looking exhausted at the end of term, strove to keep the children reasonably quiet and calm.

I tried to appear interested in every act but really I was only interested in Sam.

At last, his first appearance, with five other children, was announced and I sat up expectantly.

He was dressed in his best shirt and tie and looked a lot less nervous than I was. I just hoped he would be OK, that nothing would go wrong, that he wouldn't make a mistake, and that his new found confidence wouldn't come crashing down.

I needn't have worried. Sam kept the group going with the difficult rhythms the song entailed, and he even sang the descant on his own, while keeping the others in time. Everybody sat there, enthralled, watching Sam give a masterful performance.

We all knew that Sam had his problems with school work, but in those few moments we were entranced by this virtuoso performance, and as the last notes died away everyone broke out into spontaneous and enthusiastic applause. The good thing was that the children were applauding as hard as the adults. They knew what that performance meant and the whole audience was united in its appreciation.

Sam assumed his matter of fact look and led his group off the stage.

What's the fuss about? he seemed to be thinking, but deep down I knew he would be pleased.

But if we thought that was the end of Sam's big moment we were all wrong, as the last item of the concert involved Sam playing the drums in a band with three other children. Just when I thought that this couldn't get any better, he excelled himself with a drum solo that was just superb. I wasn't the only adult who had tears in their eyes and I felt so proud of him.

Mr Fox stood up at the end, thanked the performers, and the audience for coming, then asked us if we wanted an encore.

The deafening cheer resounded round the hall and there was obviously no doubt as to which act we wanted to hear again.

Sam took to the stage like an old pro, seated himself behind the drum kit and counted the group in.

The audience went wild and the teachers gave up any attempts to keep the children calm and seated. It didn't matter, though.

We all wanted to salute Sam, a boy who at last was good at something.

§

It was so easy to teach Sam, unlike some of my pupils. He was eager to learn, his behaviour was not a problem, and you could have a decent conversation with him. But he always had this air of detachment about him, an independent attitude which stopped us from becoming too close. It was as though he was determined to keep me at arm's length.

Some years later, when he had gone to another school, I decided to send him a Christmas card. As I was passing the school anyway, I drove in, approached the door, rang the bell, and asked if I could leave a card for him.

The very pleasant Secretary said, "Would you like me

to go and get him so that you can deliver it in person?"
"Well, yes, but I don't want to interrupt a lesson or
be a nuisance," I replied.
"No, that won't be a problem. I think he's in a
Spanish lesson, let me check."
Heck, the idea of Sam learning Spanish when he had
enough problems learning English really blew my
mind!
The Secretary bustled off and five minutes later she
returned with a rather reluctant Sam in tow. He
looked at me impassively and I knew that this was a
mistake.
"Hi, Sam!" I said cheerfully. "How are you doing?"
"Alright."
"How are your parents?"
"Alright."
"I hear that you're learning Spanish. How's that
going?"
"Alright."
"Can you say anything in Spanish for me?"
"Not really. I've forgotten a lot of it."
He stared down at his feet and never once looked me
in the eye.
This really was not going very well and he looked as
if I was the last person on earth that he wanted to see.
I really wished that I hadn't come.
"Well, I'll be going then. I hope that you have a good
Christmas and say hello to your parents as well."
"Alright."
He went back to his Spanish lesson and I stood there,
feeling quite desolate. It was as if he couldn't wait to
get away from me and his indifference had thrown
me. Hadn't he liked me before? Was it just my

imagination or hadn't we got on really well?

"Our Sam's never been one for showing his feelings, you know."

The kindly voice of the Secretary broke into my thoughts.

"I wouldn't worry. It's not you."

"No, I know you're right, but…" I tailed off. "Well, thank you, anyway." And I went back to my car before she could see the tears in my eyes.

That day taught me a lesson. When the children left me they moved on, and I had to as well, however difficult that was.

When I was a mainstream teacher of Infants I spent the whole year that they had with me trying to teach them to be independent. At the end of the school year the whole school would go into the hall and the children would be told which class they would be going into next year. At the end of the Assembly they would go with their new teacher to see their new classroom.

As they went off without a backward glance at me I would think, couldn't any of you show just a little bit of remorse about leaving me? Doesn't anybody feel sad? A few tears wouldn't go amiss!

And yet, I knew that I had done my job and I was pleased really - well, sort of pleased.

4

101 ways to crack an egg!

Dennis was a cheerful boy, aged ten, with a cheeky grin and a sense of humour to match. To my surprise he could read quite competently, although obviously not as well as his classmates. He had good phonic skills, but his writing skills were very poor. He couldn't sequence his ideas and, like most boys with Special Needs, he hated writing. So, my task was to make sequencing and writing more fun so that he could develop his skills and face a writing task without the familiar, "Oh no, I ain't doing that!"

Dennis was a pupil at Priestley Junior School, a large, rambling, antiquated stone built pile on a busy main road, and from the outside, could easily have been used as a double for Colditz PoW Camp. However, in total contrast, the interior was bright and modern. It had two floors, each with its own hall and classrooms along either side.

One day I staggered into the school with all the ingredients to make a jam sandwich. He watched in complete amazement as I produced each item from my cavernous bag.

"Cor, what are we doing today, Miss Young?"

Resisting the urge to say, "Well, Dennis, I thought that we would split the atom today and tomorrow we could find the answer to World Poverty!", I actually said, "How about making a jam sandwich?"

I paused while he yelled, "Yes!" at the top of his voice down my ear.

"Then we have to think about the different things that we did, put them in order and..." I gulped, "write about it."

"Oh no!" He looked pleadingly at me. "How about just making the jam sandwich?"

"How about I put everything away again?"

He rolled his eyes at me but suddenly acquiesced. I was one step ahead of him though.

"You can eat half the sandwich when you've done half the writing and the other half when you have finished the writing." He frowned.

"Dennis, I <u>will</u> help you. I'm not going to leave you to it."

"OK!" He grinned at me. "Let's get going - I'm starving!" (This was ten minutes after his lunch!)

I kept my promise and he stuck to his side of the bargain. After he'd wolfed down his sandwich as if he hadn't eaten for a week, he asked me if he could make another one. Well, why not? It would take me well over my forty minute slot but I knew that the teacher wouldn't mind and I could spare the time. He grinned at me, realising that his charm had won through. That day started a very fulfilling and happy time for Dennis and me. What I hadn't mentioned before was that he had a reputation for fighting and getting into trouble in the playground, and he could be troublesome in the classroom. I wanted to turn his behaviour round so that he was known as Dennis the Cook, not Dennis the troublemaker. Always aim high. That's what I say!

So, each Wednesday I would bring all the ingredients in for Dennis to cook something. (Ideally, I would have taken him shopping but there wasn't time for that.) He loved every minute of it and, as he was good company, so did I. We laughed a lot and our relationship developed into a fruitful, happy one.

The next week I took in a blender, some bananas and milk (the healthy ingredients), and three different kinds of ice-cream. Our mission that day was to create the perfect milkshake. Now, Dennis's cooking skills were non-existent, so to say that some of our sessions were unpredictable and exciting was putting it mildly. I came to realise that Dennis could write a book entitled 'One Hundred And One Ways To Break An Egg And Still Miss The Bowl.'

So the blender was definitely under my control, despite his best pleading, smiley face.

"No way, Dennis," I firmly told him and he knew that no amount of wheedling was going to change my mind. Bearing in mind the Science curriculum, we experimented all afternoon. (Our sessions on a Wednesday afternoon became longer and longer but I didn't mind as I felt that I was doing something worthwhile and enjoyable.)

As any adults and children went past our temporary kitchen they would all linger and then they wouldn't be able to resist stopping to see what we were doing.

"Mm, that smells good!"

"What are you making?"

"That looks really nice!"

"Can I have a bit, please?"

"Ooh, I wondered what that delicious smell was!"

"You can smell this all over the school!"

These positive comments all made Dennis's chest swell with pride and his self-esteem was growing.

The trouble was that they all wanted to sample what we had made. We couldn't really feed the children, not all two hundred of them, but the members of Staff soon came to expect a taste. At first it was just a select few but by the time we stopped our sessions we seemed to be feeding half the Staff, whose feedback was always very positive. Dennis became even more enthusiastic about being a Chef. The other children declared that he was an ace Chef and he couldn't have wished for a more glowing testimonial. This enthusiasm didn't carry over into his writing but you can't have everything!

Next week I thought that we would make something savoury so, still trying to keep the recipes reasonably healthy, but mindful of what children like to eat, I took in the ingredients to make turkey burgers. He was ecstatic when he heard the 'burger' bit. Each stage of the recipe involved new challenges for us both. The onion had to be grated without extra finger flavour, the egg had to be broken into a bowl (as already mentioned this was **very** tricky), and the mixture had to be shaped into identical balls and then flattened. Each one turned out totally different from its predecessor but by the eighth he was getting the idea.

While we were doing all this, children and adults were walking past, the smell of the onions and frying burgers drawing them inexorably towards us. The children particularly were very envious and Dennis was bursting with pride as he explained what he was doing. The adults were superb. They were so fulsome in their praise, so encouraging, and that was just what Dennis needed. Nearly all of my pupils had serious problems with their self-confidence and much of the bad behaviour from some of them emanated from the fact that they couldn't read or write very well like their peers, so that they felt inferior.

We had earlier realised that a cricket coach had come into the school, and he was running coaching sessions in the hall near where we were cooking. At last, about two o'clock, the burgers were cooked and Dennis had one in a bread bun in his hand, wondering if he could possibly squeeze any more fried onions and tomato sauce onto it.

The cricket coach emerged from the hall at that precise moment, looked at the burger and announced, "I haven't had any lunch yet and the smell has been driving me mad."

Dennis looked at the burger, looked at the coach, and without a word handed it over. I was so proud of him that I thought I would burst. It was a totally unselfish act and it was just as important for him to learn about putting others first as it was to learn to cook, read or write. Dennis's day was made when the coach said, "That was absolutely delicious! It's the best burger that I've ever had! Thank you very much, lad."

He then slapped a £2 coin on the table and Dennis's joy knew no bounds! The £ signs in his eyes went into overdrive! Not only was he enjoying himself but you could make money at this game too! That day really helped him to be even more generous with his cooking as I knew that sometimes sharing didn't always come easily to him.

After a while people were asking us for the recipes so our biggest venture yet was begun. I had decided that we were going to produce a Cookery book of recipes we had used together. It would be a big challenge, but one which I knew (hoped!) would boost his confidence. As I drove to the school that afternoon I smiled to myself as I imagined the reaction that I would get from Dennis as I told him about our latest project. I collected him from his classroom and tried to keep up as he bounced down the corridor. Hmm, he was obviously in a buoyant mood today!

We sat down and I waited for the inevitable, "What are we doing today Miss Young? I'm not writing anything, am I?"

"No, Dennis, not today, but I wondered how you felt about writing a book?"

"No way, Miss Young," he replied firmly, looking at me with a look that said, has she finally lost her marbles?

"Kids like me don't write books."

His cheery smile vanished from his face and he looked defeated and vulnerable.

"Well, I think that you could write a Cookery book – no, Dennis, listen to me first," I said firmly as he groaned.

"All the recipes have been written down by you already and I will type them out. Are you listening? Look at me, Dennis! THERE IS NO NEED FOR YOU TO DO ANY WRITING!"

He brightened up again and the smile returned to his face.

"I would like you just to draw some pictures to go with each recipe and leave the rest to me."

"Great! You mean I'm going to be an author?"

"Yes, Dennis, you are going to be an author!"

He enthusiastically started to do the drawings and I knew that he couldn't wait to get back to his class so that he could tell everybody.

We decided that we would sell the book to the pupils and Staff to make some money for charity. Dennis couldn't believe that he was actually going to write a book and he was very keen to see the finished product. So was I, until I realised the enormity of the actual task of printing it. However, the generosity of people never fails to amaze me, and soon the project was up and running.

My lovely husband typed up all the recipes and put them into book form. The two School Secretaries, who were great and had been very kind to me from the moment that I walked into school, gave up some of their holiday in order to photocopy and staple one hundred and twenty books.

Dennis illustrated all the recipes, wrote a foreword and designed the front cover. We only charged 25p per book. (I thought they were worth more but the Headteacher was insistent that was the most we could charge.)

The books sold, appropriately, like hot cakes and we raised £30. Even my very supportive family and friends bought them and as they were actually getting value for money I had no qualms about encouraging them to buy a book.

As the money rolled in, I decided that we needed to discuss what we were going to do with it.

Dennis thought long and hard, not something that he did very often, I'm afraid.

"The RSPCA," he declared firmly. "I like animals and they have lots to look after at the Home."

I was quite impressed at his decisiveness and his resolution, so I arranged for a very nice lady to come to a School Assembly and in front of everyone Dennis presented her with a cheque. The whole school, children and adults alike, applauded him for quite some time and he stood there lapping it all up with a huge grin on his face. He had learnt to cook, had improved his Literacy skills, his Numeracy skills, Design and Artistic skills, learnt about Science and Marketing, to be less selfish, and most of all his self-esteem had shot up and, as I had hoped, the children now knew him as Dennis the Cook. Job done! Here is one of Dennis' recipes as written down by him (with only a little help from me!)

Dennis's Gingerbread Snakes

Ingredients

100g plain flour	50g margarine
100g oatmeal	½ egg, beaten
1 teaspoon ground ginger	100g caster sugar
1 tablespoon dark syrup	1 tablespoon milk

Currants and peel for decoration

Method
1. Wash your hands.
2. Put on your apron.
3. Put the flour, oatmeal, ginger, and caster sugar into the bowl and rub in the margarine until it looks like breadcrumbs.
4. Mix the syrup with the egg and the milk.
5. Pour this into the bowl and mix into a paste.
6. Shape into snakes and decorate with currants and peel for eyes and mouths.
7. Put on a greased baking tray with a good gap between each one.
8. Bake in the oven at 180 C/350 F for 15-20 minutes.

However, not all of my times with Dennis were as pleasurable.

His class was to go out on a trip to Malham Cove in the Yorkshire Dales and his teacher asked if I would like to go with them. This would be really handy for all involved as I could keep an eye on Dennis, hopefully stop him from becoming too boisterous, and the teachers wouldn't have to worry about who was going to supervise him. It wasn't easy but I managed to rearrange my hours with my other pupils and I duly agreed to go.

Now, while some teachers love going out on trips, many don't. It is a heck of a responsibility as the outside world is full of dangers and risks, and Year Six boys can be a bit of a handful.

In the old days, ie thirty years ago we just took the children out, without worrying about risk assessments, and Health and Safety. We used our common sense, planned accordingly and, as long as we had plenty of parental help, off we went. Now **there's** another thing to think about - which parents do you take?

Don't get me wrong, most of the parents I took with me were lovely, sensible and reliable, but I did have one who kept nipping off for a crafty smoke, and another who gave out sweets like they were going to be rationed again - not a good idea when there was a long coach journey to be endured! When I took Infants out there was always one who was ill and it didn't help that I was often feeling rather sick myself, as I didn't travel well by coach in those days. The opposite situation occurred when I took a father with me. Now, this was unheard of but gradually, with people working more flexibly, more men started to volunteer to help in schools. In my last school I had a fantastic team of helpers who worked mainly on Literacy computer programs with the children but Alec, the only man, said that he would be very happy to play Maths games and help the children in that way. The children loved him! They loved all the helpers, but some of the boys particularly enjoyed talking to a man. There aren't that many men working in Primary Schools and, let's face it, nowadays many children don't have a stable male role model in their lives.

Anyway, this particular Dad who came on the trip with us was very good and obviously took his job seriously - how seriously I realised when, after he'd gone, I found a list he had made of all the children in his group with a detailed description of each one, and I mean detailed.

So, you'll probably have realised by now that I came into the category of teachers who didn't like going out on trips. I think one little girl summed it up once when she said at the end of a long trip, "Mrs Young, you've spent all day just counting us." An observant child that and indeed she was quite right.

I thank God that in all my years of teaching I never lost a child on a trip, or for that matter, none of my pupils ever died. That may sound a bit melodramatic but it does happen and the thought of attending the funeral of a child I had taught just sends shivers down my spine even now.

To get back to Dennis, I knew that he could be a bit of a handful but we got on well so everything should be fine, shouldn't it? Oh, how naïve I was!

The first problem was that he didn't have a packed lunch, but teachers are usually prepared for most things and we always took too much for our own lunch just in case, so after a whip round that problem was solved. He probably got rather more than he bargained for in the way of healthy food, but at least he wouldn't go hungry!

I sat near him on the coach, but not next to him, as I didn't want him to feel that he had been singled out for special treatment. The problems started when we arrived, got off the coach, and the children were handed a worksheet to complete as they went round. The questions were quite complicated; in fact I'm not sure that I knew all the answers, although we were reassured that every answer would be found on an Information Board. This didn't bode well for Dennis though. He wouldn't be able to read it for a start and I could already see from the look on his face and his body language that he was not happy.

If I had known that there was going to be such a difficult worksheet, or indeed, any worksheet at all, I could have prepared an easier one for Dennis, in the same format, so nobody would have been able to see the difference at a glance. Ah well, hindsight is a wonderful thing and I had to think of something now. But, it was too late.

Those first few minutes had dented his confidence so much, and when that happened and he realised that everybody else could do it, there was one inevitable outcome. It was no good me pointing out that other children were being helped by adults so what was wrong with me helping him?

No, he had gone too far into his feelings of total

inadequacy, so in Dennis's mind he was going to have to seize some power back and reassert himself. He was very awkward all morning but I was just about controlling him and there had been no major incidents. We settled down for our picnic lunch quite early on. You have to eat early on a school trip because there are only so many cries of, "Can we have our lunch now?" any teacher can endure, particularly as the first one comes as the coach draws away from the school gates.

As soon as he had finished his lunch Dennis jumped up and started to prowl around. His meal hadn't been quite to his taste but he was lucky to get anything at all.

We were sitting at the bottom of the huge, towering cliff with the sheer face and nearby were the steps leading up to a limestone pavement. At the edge of the pavement was a sheer drop. Dennis suddenly set off up the steps at a rate of knots, knowing that these were out of bounds at the moment, particularly without an adult. I threw my sandwich down and hurtled past the other Staff who, concentrating on their own group of children, hadn't seen where he had gone.

They stared in amazement as I started to climb the steps as fast as I could. Dennis could be so impetuous and unpredictable that I knew he could do anything when he reached the top, especially anything that involved sheer rock faces and edges.

Now, the thing was, that apart from being nearly forty years older than Dennis, I have asthma as well, so after a few seconds of trying to keep up with him my chest was pounding and my lungs felt as if they were going to burst. I don't know how I did it, but

I reached the top shortly after he did. It is amazing what fear and trepidation can make you do! I knew that if I shouted at him not to go near the edge he would do just that, so, while trying to catch my breath, I wandered over to him and said casually,

"You get a great view up here, don't you, Dennis. Let's see what we can see, shall we? Oh look, there's the rest of the class, and can you see that house over there? How many sheep do you think there are in that field down there? It's a lovely day, isn't it? Oh, look, somebody's waving at us! Who do you think it is? Aren't we lucky that it's not raining?"

I rabbited on in this vein for quite some time, being painfully aware of my fear of heights, as well as my inability to breathe properly.

Dennis gave me an old-fashioned look then walked even nearer to the edge. I looked around furtively, thinking that surely somebody would come up to help me. The Staff told me later that they thought Dennis and I were just doing our own thing! Just as I had given up all hope of getting him down safely, he turned and started to run towards the steps. Oh no, not again! Well, this time it was slightly easier going down, but not a lot and I arrived at the bottom, only just behind Dennis, but even more out of breath.

"Hi, Dennis, do you want a kickabout?" shouted one of his mates. The teachers had thoughtfully brought a few footballs so that the children could use up a bit of energy, and boy, was I pleased!

Dennis shot off towards his friends and I slumped down on the grass.

"By, Pam, you're fit, aren't you?" His teacher smiled at me. She was a good twenty years younger than me.

"I don't think that I could have run up and down those steps like that!"

I smiled, but said nothing. I was incapable of speech at that particular moment and for a few moments after that!

Really, I could sympathise with Dennis. It is a fact, but not all adults realise this, that when a young child misbehaves it is usually because he/she is trying to tell us something, and doesn't have the verbal skills to tell us what the problem is. It might be something as short-lived as tiredness or hunger. Usually parents recognise this and can remedy the situation.

But long-term and more persistent bad behaviour is often the result of a child feeling unloved, lacking attention, or being made to feel a failure with the inevitable feelings of frustration.

Imagine sitting day after day, hour after hour in a lesson where the teacher might as well be speaking Chinese, and the written word might as well be in a foreign language. The situation is made even worse when everybody else seems to understand every word and can do everything that the teacher asks. How would that make you feel? Some children with-draw into themselves but many more misbehave and in that situation nobody wins. The child, the teacher and fellow pupils all suffer as the teacher tries to cope with a disruptive pupil.

The National Curriculum has not done these children any favours as the lessons go too fast for them and there is never any time for them to catch up. I'm talking about the children who have significant learning problems now, not those who would benefit from an intervention strategy.

Put the money into helping these children with severe problems and you could improve behaviour in schools, and reduce the prison population. It is a fact that many prisoners cannot read or write properly. Doesn't that tell us something?

5

If You Can't Stand The Heat…

I'm afraid that not all of my associations with the Statemented children were successful. The children with behaviour problems, and I must say that we are mainly talking about boys, were a real challenge. Some of them were a huge problem in class but were reasonably behaved with me, one of the reasons being that they enjoyed the one-to-one situation, and they saw my room as a sanctuary away from the pressures of the National Curriculum. Ah, the joys of the Literacy Hour!

We need to listen to children, but when they can't express themselves and say how they are feeling, we need to observe them. They cannot express their feelings vocally, so they do it through their behaviour. I can't emphasise this enough.

Although the Government would say that it puts intervention strategies in at an early stage, these usually do not help the really disadvantaged children who often get very little help and support from home. It was always so difficult to get one-to-one specialist help for these children, and yet thousands of pounds would have to be spent later on trying to cope with their bad behaviour.

Having said that, I question the way that we start teaching children formally so early on in their school careers. Many countries in Europe don't start to do this until the children are seven years old, while we start bombarding them with assessments and tests when they are four years old. Children are subject to a lot of pressure in our schools nowadays and they know this, and I feel sorry for them.

I liked school when I was a child, particularly my Primary School. My Headmaster, as they were called in those days, was pretty fearsome if a child stepped out of line, but not many did because we had the deterrent of 'the bat'. It wasn't as fearsome as the cane but, as only the boys found out, it could really hurt! If you were misbehaving in class by talking or not paying attention you were likely to have a piece of chalk come whistling past your ear, and that soon brought you back to reality.

If it was a lovely day we were all taken on a nature walk and I can still identify many wild flowers, birds and insects today because of his enthusiasm and interest. Many children today don't know what a daffodil is, yet they have to learn about the Rain Forest because of the National Curriculum. What about learning about our flora and fauna first?

When York suffered from very bad flooding a few years ago, I questioned a teacher about why they weren't doing a project on it; after all, the children were interested and were affected by it.

The answer came back, "No time - the work is all planned for the term and I have to get through it." See what I mean? And, again, I do not blame the teachers for this.

§

I once had to lead a staff meeting in order to inform the teachers about the new Special Educational Needs Code. I decided to try to show them what it was like for many of my children in their classes. I showed them, on the overhead projector, a passage of Russian writing, which I then asked them to read and answer some questions which I had written down for them; things like 'What was the girl's name? Where was she going?'

Now, one of the teachers was a linguist and had some knowledge of the Russian language, so I had talked to her beforehand and she was prepared for this. As I finished telling the teachers what I wanted them to do - and of course they had no chance of doing it - this teacher started to write the answers down.

The reactions of the other teachers were interesting. The ones on either side of the teacher who was writing looked panic-stricken and tried to look at her answers. If children did this in one of their lessons they would be bawled out. A couple of the women tried to do their best by guessing the answers. They knew that Natasha was a Russian name so they wrote that down. At least they had a go! Some just stared at me in disbelief that I had the audacity to ask them to do something that they were unable to do. Hmm, wasn't that what happened to my children every day? But the most interesting reaction was mainly from the men, it has to be said.

They folded their arms, while some swung back on their chairs, looked at me defiantly and said things like, "I'm not doing that!" A couple of them then started to get really stroppy and to misbehave when I told them that they had to do it. I paused dramatically and then announced that what they had experienced was what my pupils went through every day, and that they felt just as I had made the teachers feel. I would like to think that this made a difference to their teaching but I recognized that they were under pressure from the demands of league tables and the National Curriculum so that, with the best will in the world, they couldn't really change much. Still, at least they knew how it felt to have Special Needs in the Literacy Hour!

§

One child who will forever stay in my mind (I'm being careful here not to say that I failed with him) was a junior boy, very tall for his age, called Alex. I emphasise his size, because he strutted round that school as if he owned the place. He was ten years old when I met him and already his reputation had gone before him. He had no respect for adults and knew no boundaries. His fair hair and angelic looks belied the fact that he was the cheekiest child I ever taught and he feared no-one.

He was being brought up by his older sister who was only nineteen years old herself. Their Dad wasn't on the scene and hadn't been for many years, and his Mum was in and out of hospital. His sister was doing her best but really couldn't get to grips with his behaviour, and nobody blamed her for that.

He probably had Dyslexia - we weren't sure because he was very difficult to assess - but he was certainly very much behind his peers. Having said that, he was extremely quick in arguments, giving excuses, and being generally cheeky, but he couldn't seem to grasp that he wasn't going to get very far in life with those character traits.

However, I like a challenge so when his Statement came through I accepted the task of teaching him basic Literacy skills. He wasn't too bad to start with and my sense of humour was, as usual, a big help in getting him to co-operate. So were the ~~bribes~~, sorry, rewards of my toy bag and stickers. Gradually it became harder and harder to motivate him and he became more and more unco-operative.

One day, in the staff room, Sue, his Class Teacher, noticed me taking two pain relief tablets.

"Oh dear, have you got a headache?" she asked me.

"No," I heard myself admitting, "not yet, but I know that I will have when I've taught Alex."

The look on her face said it all and I knew then that I was on a downward spiral to becoming ill if something didn't change. I began to dread his lessons and I was lying awake at night thinking of what I could do with him.

Then one day I went to collect him from his class room. By this time he had a male teacher who I knew was struggling to cope with him, as we all did. As I knocked and entered the classroom I noticed that Alex's chair was empty. Oh yes - could he be away? Please, please let him be away! But children like Alex are never away so I didn't get my hopes up. Sure enough, the teacher just pointed to a corner of the classroom, and there I spied Alex crouching, like a wild animal, with a thunderous look on his face. If I could have turned and run away without losing my professionalism, I would have done.

"Alex is having a few problems today!" said his tattered-looking teacher.

"Yes," I thought, "that's stating the flaming obvious, isn't it!"

Now Alex had never refused to come down to my

room before. In fact, like most of my pupils, he welcomed the chance to escape from the classroom.

So, I approached him confidently, feeling rather sorry for him as he crouched there in front of all his classmates, and thinking that if I could take him out of that situation I could help him. I held out my hand and took hold of his, but instead of coming willingly, he jerked his arm back and almost pulled my arm out of its socket.

I then had a dilemma. I didn't want to lose face in front of all his classmates who were now avidly watching the situation unfold, and I had to get him down to my room so that I could teach him. A tad optimistic maybe! Consoling words went unheeded but the teacher and I managed to get him out of the classroom, and then he reluctantly came to my room. There, he was his usual awkward self and we had a difficult lesson, though I had mentally adjusted his targets for that session, and didn't expect to get much work out of him. The problem had all stemmed from an argument he and the Class Teacher had had and I got the fallout!

Next morning I could hardly get out of bed. My shoulder and neck were very painful, and just picking up my school bags or reversing the car were almost impossible. I staggered into school and saw Alex's teacher in the staff room. He took note of the state I was in, and unbeknown to me, went to tell the Headteacher, Mr Wilson.

Meanwhile, I had gone to collect my first pupil, Shona, who was no bother and we got on famously. She saw that I was having difficulty moving and lifting things, and was quite happy to help me in any way she could. We were sitting working together when suddenly the door flew open, without any warning, and Mr Wilson appeared in the doorway with an angry look on his face.

"What are you doing in school?" he barked at me. I could feel the tears coming to my eyes as I looked at him blankly.

"Alex's teacher told me what happened yesterday. You're injured and you should be at home."

He then seemed to realise that Shona was sitting there, drinking in every detail.

"Shona, off you go back to your classroom," he said firmly.

Shona was on the verge of saying, "What, and miss all the fun?" but she had the sense to realise that he was being serious.

When she'd gone he announced, "Come down to the Office and fill in an accident form and then you're going home."

I managed to find my tongue at last.

"No, I'm fine," I said with as much conviction as I could manage, which wasn't much.

One look from him and I hauled myself to my feet and went down to the Office to fill in the accident form, with Mr Wilson standing over me, telling me what to put. Then, before the tears really came, I went home, took some painkillers and slept for the rest of the day.

Alex hadn't meant to hurt me, I knew that, but it was a while before I was completely recovered, although I was back at school the next day.

§

My relationship with Alex went up and down from day to day. He showed great interest in a cross-stitch picture I was doing, liked to see its progress and even brought me some threads. On other days he would be so awkward and I came to feel that I was being ground down.

The final straw came when one day he was in a really bad mood.

"Is there a problem, Alex?" I enquired solicitously. "Because if there is, let's try to sort it out."

"Yeah, there is a problem," he snapped back at me. "It's you - it's like talking to a brick wall."

I knew at that moment that I had had enough. All the stresses and strains of the last weeks and months culminated in that one moment of revelation. Why should I put myself through this? I'd never been a very decisive person, but my mind was suddenly very clear and I knew that I couldn't cope with him anymore. Somebody else would just have to take over from me before I was really ill.

It's hard to explain how difficult it can be to teach one small boy who looked so angelic, but believe me it could be soul-destroying.

At lunch time I went to find the SENCo (Special Educational Needs Co-ordinator) to tell her that I was throwing in the towel. She didn't try to question my decision as she knew how hard I had found him. She called a meeting with the Educational Psychologist, Tony, who asked me if I wanted to stop teaching Alex and if so, when.

"Yes, and now," I said with determination and relief. Another Tutor was brought in for the last few weeks of term. She found him to be very difficult and said that if she hadn't been able to see the end she wouldn't have taken him on. Alex was transferred to a Specialist Unit.

He was expelled soon after. Years later I came across him again. He hadn't changed at all. At least some of my self-confidence was restored when I realised that nobody had had much success with him anywhere. I daren't think what has happened to him now that he has left school, but I think that my worst fears will have been realised.

§

Another boy had been abused as a very young child and I was convinced that he had AD/HD as well. The thing was that he was very bright, and as my job was to help children with learning difficulties, and as his behaviour became more and more challenging, to use the modern day terminology, I felt that I shouldn't be there, and that the money used to pay me would be better spent in supporting his lovely teacher in the classroom.

I struggled on, but came to dread my sessions with him. In fact, ten years later I still get a feeling of dread if I drive past the school.

As before with Alex, I found myself lying awake at night, wondering what I was going to do with him. The headaches had returned and I could see history repeating itself.

The crunch came when he swung back on the back two legs of his chair then swung forward, trying to get the chair leg to land on my foot. I quickly moved my foot out of the way but that was it. This was just the final episode in a long and difficult relationship and enough was enough.

But this was the second time that I was giving up on a child. Did that mean that I was a failure? Well, in my book, yes it did, despite all the reassurances that my husband and friends tried to give me. Perhaps I ought to give up the job?

I went to see my Line Manager, Ann, who was so kind and sympathetic and managed to convince me that I wasn't a failure!

A meeting was called and I tried to assume an air of confidence as I entered the room where the meeting was to be held. I needed all my acting skills that day as I felt sick with nerves and the sense of failure.

I couldn't believe it when all the experts agreed with me that he didn't need learning support, and that the money would be better spent on increasing the hours of his Inclusion Support Assistant.

I thought that they would probably replace me with a much more competent Tutor who would make a success of the job.

I looked round at them all.

"Why didn't anybody say this before?" I enquired.

"Well, we were waiting for you to say something," came the reply.

I could have wept! All that struggling had been for nothing! Still, it taught me a lesson and after that I wasn't quite so reticent about my pupils.

I heard later that he was doing reasonably well at Comprehensive School so at least there was a happier ending there.

6

Here Be Dragons!

I was asked to take Peter on just for a few weeks, as he was almost certainly going to a Special Language Unit in another school. It was acknowledged that he was a difficult child with many problems but, as my boss, Sue said, "It won't be for long, Pam, and you would be helping us out."

Four years later I said goodbye to Peter knowing that I had done my best and that he would move on to a mainstream school. What I didn't know then was that he would win prizes at their Speech Day, but that is jumping ahead a bit.

It could all have been so different, as our first session together was so horrendous. That night after our evening meal my husband said, "Come on, out with it, you look really worried!"

"I'm not worried so much as exhausted! There is no way that I am going to take Peter on. He was just so difficult. I had no control over him and he just ran rings round me!"

"So, what are you going to do? Are you going to ring Sue up and tell her?"

"Well, I'll just take him for the next two weeks, then he'll be going to the Special Unit."

Richard smiled, well, grimaced really, as he had an idea that this was not going to be the outcome.

Peter had Autism, language and learning difficulties, and very low self-esteem. He was terrified, and I mean terrified, of anything new so I, as a new person in his life with new ideas, ways of working, games etc was seen as a huge threat. His behaviour was awful and during that first session I had no control over him. It wasn't helpful that we had to work in the canteen with all the attendant noise and distractions, as there wasn't a proper room available. This was a frequent problem in my job and sometimes part of my half hour slot with a child would be spent in looking for a room.

I became quite used to working in cupboards - large cupboards, I grant you, but still cupboards - or in corridors, or having to move half way through a lesson as somebody else needed that space.

I was once asked to find a room for a colleague from the SEN department in York who was coming to teach some sessions at the school where I was on the Staff. She walked into the room, then headed for the stock cupboard.

"Where are you going, Sheila?" I enquired with a look of bewilderment on my face.

"Well," she admitted sheepishly, "I'm usually put in a cupboard so I naturally assumed that I would be working in one this time!" She was bowled over to be told that she could use the whole classroom!

Anyway, back to Peter who was so difficult that first session that I was worn out and very dispirited when I, with great relief, took him back to his teacher.

Now, fortunately for me, it was Peter's birthday soon after I started teaching him and, knowing that he had an obsession with trains, I bought him a card with Thomas the Tank Engine on it. Bullseye!

He was absolutely fascinated by the card and he seemed to relax and view me as a friend rather than an enemy. I wouldn't say that everything was plain sailing after that, but it was a turning point and things gradually became easier.

Birthday cards have been very important in my job and I always made the effort to remember all my pupils' birthdays. Although the children were not always very effusive and many seemed quite offhand I knew that the cards were important. One boy called Steve looked seriously at his card, as if studying it intently, then asked, "How much did this cost?"

I was quite taken aback and said gently, "That doesn't matter, Steve. I wanted to buy you a card because I like you and I want to celebrate your birthday with you." His reply was so unexpected and sad that it still gives me goose pimples after all these years.

"Don't spend your money on me, Mrs Young. I'm not worth it." Gulp.

I always asked the children who worked in the same group or twosome to sign the card for the birthday girl or boy, as I felt it was part of the 'hidden curric-ulum', doing something for somebody else. No child ever refused to sign a card and, in fact, they were always very pleased to be asked.

§

I was asked to have another pupil to work with Peter as she also had difficulties with Literacy. A girl called Susannah, she was a most delightful child, a very good role model for Peter, and a sympathetic glance from her when Peter was being difficult could really help.

As well as being a virtual non-reader, Peter refused to write anything and I had to be so patient and gentle with him, gradually building up his self-confidence.

The trouble was that I was doing too good a job! After a few weeks Peter seemed to be settling down and beginning to learn, and the decision was made to leave him in the mainstream school, with me giving additional tuition for two and a half hours per week. "Would you be willing to take him on?" Sue asked me. I opened my mouth to say that I thought that it was only temporary.

"You're doing such a good job," she continued, knowing exactly how to get round me. So, that was that, and I must say that, although we had a roller-coaster of a time together, I look back on Peter with much fondness and satisfaction.

The way to get Peter to work was through games, as with many children, and I spent a lot of time making games and personalising them.

Susannah was great and a superb role model because she never minded losing and was quite philosophical about it! If Peter lost it was a major catastrophe and he would then sink into a trough of deep despair. Occasionally there are times when I think it is right to manipulate things so that a child wins a game, but on the whole I think that they have to learn to be a good and generous loser. When Susannah or I lost we would say things like, "Never mind, I enjoyed that game!"

"Well, it's not the end of the world, is it?"

"I don't mind if I don't win!"

One day Peter lost a game and Susannah and I braced ourselves for the tears and despair. Instead, there was the faint glimmer of a smile and he said grudgingly, "Well, I suppose it's not the end of the world, is it?" Susannah and I whooped with delight and we heaped praise on him.

"Give over, you're embarrassing me!" he said, but we couldn't help ourselves, we were so thrilled. I was glad that Susannah had been there.

The first time that Peter wrote a sentence on his own was another time of celebration, and so we went on with them both improving considerably with their reading, spelling and writing. But it was not all plain sailing.

One day Peter came out of his class in a terrible mood, as if he had all the cares of the world on his shoulders. I got him back to my room, abandoned all hope of getting any work done, and gently asked him to tell me what was wrong.

"Nothing!" came the answer.

There was no possibility of saying, "That's obviously not right, Peter, now tell me what's wrong."

Eventually, after much persuasive talk, promises of treats, and gentle handling, he broke down.

Through his tears he managed to tell me that his class was going to the theatre to see a play based on The Hobbit, and he didn't want to go. Now, every other child in that class couldn't wait to go, but a classic symptom of his condition was that he hated new things.

"I won't know what to do!" he sobbed, refusing to look at me, and even turning his back on me.

So, every day leading up to the theatre visit we practised what would happen. We re-arranged the chairs in my room into a 'coach' so that he could practise getting on and sitting down in his place, while I pretended to be his teacher and gave a running commentary. The fact that his teacher was a male caused much hilarity as I did my best to impersonate him but that all added to the fun!

We practised getting off, then I re-arranged the chairs so that they were like the seats in a theatre. We practised finding our seats, sitting down and watching the stage (a table). I emphasised that he just had to sit there until the show finished, then get up and follow his teacher out.

We then practised standing up, leaving the theatre and getting on the coach.

Now, the ideal thing would have been for me to go with him, but I had commitments at other schools so this was not possible. If only I had known what would happen!

The day after the theatre visit I saw his teacher, Simon, in the staff room and asked him how the trip had gone.

"Well," he said, grinning, "not quite according to plan. There was a dragon in the show that shot out flames which set fire to the stage curtains, and we all had to be evacuated!"

"Oh no!" I gasped, "but I told Peter to sit there until the show was over. How did you manage to get him out?"

"Don't worry," Simon said. "He came willingly with me and everything was fine. It will be interesting to see what he says to you about it."

I went to get Peter as soon as I could. "Did you enjoy the show?" I asked impassively.

"Oh yes, it was great!" came the reply. "The best bit was when the dragon set fire to the curtains! That was ace!"

I could have hugged him! Another hurdle overcome!

When it was time for Peter to leave me I think that he felt a bit sad. I know that I certainly did.

One day, near the end of term, he said to me as I collected him from his classroom, "I've got a secret!"

"Oh?" I tried to look impassive.

"Yes, my Mum said not to tell you!"

"Well, you'd better not tell me then!"

He looked wistfully at me.

"It's a nice surprise!"

"Good, but don't spoil it!"

"I hope that you like it. We chose it specially."

"Peter, give over! I'm not listening!" I laughed and he smiled.

"We've got you a present!" he whispered.

"Peter, if you say one more word, I shall take you back to the class right now! And there won't be a sticker!"

I knew that would do it and it did.

Later that morning there was a knock on the door and Peter and his Mum came in. Peter was grinning from ear to ear. He presented me with a present that was beautifully wrapped and quite heavy.

"Be careful not to drop it!" Peter's Mum said hastily. "I don't know how we've got it here in one piece as Peter insisted on carrying it!"

I gingerly put it on my table and tore off the paper. Inside was a box, and inside that was a lovely Lladro figure of a boy sitting at a desk.

I nearly dropped it then, as I was so surprised by the generosity and thought that had gone into this present.

"We thought that it would remind you of Peter whenever you look at it. Thank you so much for everything that you have done for him."

That piece of Lladro is still in our lounge and is indeed a very precious memory of the boy I nearly didn't teach.

7

A New School Cook

Darren came to me with a ready-made work partner called Baz. In character they were very different, yet they got on really well, probably due to Baz's easy-going attitude and sense of fun. Darren had had a brain tumour which had left him with significant learning difficulties, enough to warrant him having a Statement. There are sometimes other associated problems with brain tumours and Darren certainly had a short fuse.

It was a case of Little and Large with those two. Darren was quite tall and stocky, whereas Baz was small and thin, and looked as though a puff of wind would blow him away. They both had lovely smiles, the only difference being that, while Baz was always grinning and larking about, Darren's smiles were not as frequent. It was a pity really, as his whole face lit up when he let himself go and forgot to scowl.

The two boys were in the class of an NQT (Newly Qualified Teacher) called Rebecca. She and I became friends immediately. She had a tough class and I like to think that I helped her when I could to get through that first year. She, in turn, provided me with support, friendship, and most importantly, lots of laughs. Even when she left to teach in Lincolnshire we remained in touch and it was a joy to go to her wedding some years later.

§

One of the good things about my job was that most of my pupils came with a Pupil Support Assistant who worked with the child in the classroom, and this was the case with Darren. Chris, as she was called, was a lovely lady, and we hit it off straight away. I have worked with many lovely Assistants who are still firm friends, and who provided me with support and encouragement.

The Assistants would put in many hours of unpaid work, either working with the child when needed, making resources, researching some other ways of helping their charges, or attending meetings. I valued their opinions greatly and in particular they could be a great source of information on the child's background. When you're feeling low and thinking that you're making no difference to the child's life at all, it is a great relief to unburden yourself to someone who understands and can boost your confidence.

Anyway, back to Darren and Baz. As in the case of Peter and Susannah, Baz provided me with much needed relief and support when Darren was being particularly awkward. He certainly had his moods, but at other times he could be pleasant and chatty and you could have a laugh with him.

Darren had a love of animals and as a result he decided to become a vegetarian, although he couldn't always say the word!

He once went on a residential course for three days and came back full of it. He was very keen to tell us about it and I always allowed the children to talk about anything to me. Baz and I listened patiently to him until the answer came to my question, "What did you have for breakfast? Was it a cooked meal?"

"Bacon and sausages, tomatoes and eggs - brilliant!" he enthused. "The breakfasts were my favourite!"

Given that Darren claimed to be a vegetarian, Baz raised his eyebrows at me and grinned. I couldn't help but grin back and raise my eyebrows too!

"But Darren, I thought that you were a vegetarian!" queried Baz, echoing my thoughts.

"I am," declared Darren impatiently, "except for sausages and bacon!"

Fortunately Darren saw the funny side of it, and Baz and I realised that we could relax and laugh with him.

§

Sometimes the children in my charge didn't do the national tests when they were eleven years old, and to try to make up for the fact that he was feeling different from the other children, I promised Darren that we would cook together, on our own as Baz was doing the tests. We decided to cook Chocolate Crunch, a type of biscuit, which doesn't need any baking. Cooking with Darren was quite an adventure, but not quite as much of an adventure as when I worked in a Nursery once on supply.

I was making Gingerbread Men with twenty four children aged three and four, in groups of six. The Nursery Assistant had provided me with a cutter which cut off all the arms and legs so these had to be stuck on individually!

I was becoming quite harassed, but was just about coping, when the Educational Psychologist arrived and insisted on discussing one of the children with me as I did this. The child's mental state was giving us cause for alarm. Yeah, well I knew how the child felt at that precise moment!

A New School Cook

Anyway, Darren's often impetuous and impatient behaviour made for a fraught lesson, but we got there and he looked proudly at the biscuits. I always encouraged the children to share what they made and, despite Darren's disappointment in the fact that he wasn't going to eat all sixteen biscuits in one go, he eventually acquiesced and I let him choose to whom he would give the results of his labours. Baz was an obvious choice, Simon, his teacher, Mrs Jones, his Teaching Assistant, and surprisingly the School Cook were among his recipients.

All the people were very encouraging and praised him a lot, especially as I was miming, out of sight of Darren, that they were OK to eat as he had been well-supervised. Darren's self-esteem was going up and up, and as the Cook tasted it, I thought he was going to burst with pride when she said, "You know, this is so good that I would like to put it on our menu and I would like you to make it and serve it!"

Darren beamed at her, then turned to me and yelled, "Yeah! Can I, Miss Young, can I?"

My first thoughts went along the lines of 'Health and Safety', 'Fire', 'Kitchen burning down' etc, etc but at the same time all I could think of to say was, "I'll see what I can do, Darren, but I can't promise you anything."

Later on I returned to talk to Carol, the Cook. I voiced my concerns to her, but she dismissed them. I then asked her, "What do you think Margaret (the Headteacher) would say? Do you think that she would give permission?"

"No, probably not," she admitted, "so you'll have to work on that one, won't you?"

I knew that Darren's self-esteem would go sky high if he could do this and I would do anything to help with that so…

A few days later, having checked with the Secretary about the Headteacher's diary for that day, I went to Carol, the Cook, and said nonchalantly, "Margaret's out this morning - all morning."

"Is she?" said Carol, looking very interested. "Is Darren here today?"

"Yes, he is," I said. There was a pause.

"Right, bring him along as soon as you can and we'll get started."

Yes, I know it was a bit underhand and I was taking a risk but if you could have seen the joy on Darren's face as he served out the biscuits that he had made to the children - well, I think that most people would have done the same.

I did actually take a photograph of him with the two Cooks. He is dressed the same as them in an overall and hat and it is one of the most treasured mementoes of my teaching career. It was all thanks to a School Cook who was prepared to go that extra mile, too, for the sake of a child.

§

Darren was a boy who was a good lad at heart but his impulsive behaviour, feelings of low self-esteem and frustration, and the fact that he was easily led by more devious children, often led him into situations where he did the wrong thing. But, give him a simple job to do and he was a different boy.

We had a lot of planted troughs around the school and

obviously they all needed watering when the weather was dry. Darren was given this job and he carried it out as if his life depended on it. As soon as he had eaten his dinner he would collect his watering can from the staff room and off he would go, usually followed by a group of inquisitive Infants. He would answer their questions patiently and calmly, whereas other Year Six boys might have got a bit fed up.

Not only did this make him feel important and good about himself, but it also ensured that he was kept out of mischief.

I firmly believed, right through my teaching career, that, once given a simple job to do, many naughty children flourished, and their behaviour improved. Not all teachers agreed with me and some felt that such a child could never be trusted in any situation.

I once entrusted the job of putting the teachers' chairs away after Assembly to a boy who was becoming a problem. He was doing the job very efficiently when the Headteacher spotted him, assumed the worst and told him to stop it and get out.

§

Baz was a very friendly, cheerful boy with very good manners and an outgoing personality. He was marvellous as a role model for Darren, and a bit of light relief for me when Darren was having a bad day. He was the kind of friend that I wished Darren would hang around with.

Having sung Baz's praises to my husband, he saw what I meant when we went to the cinema one day. As we were going up the stairs to take our seats, we saw Baz and one of his mates coming down, obviously filling in time as we were all very early. We passed the time of day, introductions were made, then we carried on upstairs.

Now, being a romantic and loving couple, we usually sit near the back row so that we can cuddle up to each other. Imagine our surprise when Baz and his friend suddenly loomed up out of the semi-light, and Baz enquired politely, "Do you mind if we sit next to you?"

We leapt away from each other while I muttered, "No, of course we don't mind!"

Not strictly true, I must admit, but although the boys cramped our style, we were rather flattered that they wanted to sit near us! Yes, I know that the more cynical amongst you will be thinking that they did it deliberately to annoy us but, knowing Baz, I don't honestly think that that was the case. Or am I being very naïve?

Talking of my husband, I don't think that I could have done such a demanding job without his support. He was always very discreet, and never talked to anyone else about my pupils. I knew that I could trust him, and it helped that he didn't have a loose tongue. There were many times when I just needed to offload when I was worried about a child, or found myself in a difficult situation. He would listen carefully, and I knew that he was listening and not just saying, "Yes, dear."

He would offer advice when it was needed and keep quiet when it wasn't.

Then again he would rejoice with me when I had a breakthrough with a child, even though it would often seem, to an outsider, that it was a very, very small breakthrough.

He often made me pieces of apparatus in order to help a child with their learning. Once, he designed and made a device which would only show one line at a time of a printed page, to help a boy who had problems with his sight, after having had an operation to remove a brain tumour. He spent ages on it and it did the trick but the boy had behaviour problems as well and he refused to use it.

When the children reached milestones in their learning, he taught me how to make them a certificate on the computer, using their preferences for the pictures. At the end of term, when I assessed each child to see how many of the Literacy keywords they could read and spell, he again helped to make certificates. All the children were asked what picture they wanted, and many an evening we trawled the Internet looking for exactly the right illustration. The children treasured these certificates, and parents and teachers would say what a difference they made to their self-esteem. Most kept them in a special file at their home, as a permanent reminder of their success.

Most of the children were quite willing for the certificates to be presented in a whole school Assembly by the Headteachers, who were always willing to bolster the self-confidence of their pupils. The other children would clap and cheer, for many of them realised the effort that had gone into achieving their new total, and the recipients would glow with pride, and I'm sure would grow an extra inch!

However, there is always an exception that proves the rule, and this was Baz. When I checked with him about getting his certificate in front of the whole school he looked decidedly uneasy.

"I'd rather not," he declared firmly. "I don't want to be rude, and you know that I like coming to you, but I don't want the whole school to know that I'm not very good at reading."

I opened my mouth, but he went on, "Yes, I know that I'm getting better but I'm still not that great, am I?"

Big as he was I wanted to hug him but of course I wouldn't have dared.

"No, that's fine, Baz," I said. "It's your choice and I wouldn't make you do anything that you don't want to do."

He smiled. "As long as you understand that I do like coming here."

You couldn't fault Baz's manners and his caring nature.

"I understand perfectly and it's fine, honestly."

He didn't change his mind even when he saw the applause that the others received. I respected him for that.

8

Snails, Woodlice and Butterflies

Sharon was a very sad little girl. She had had a terrible early childhood and she was only six years old when I met her. She was living with a foster mother who was doing a brilliant job looking after her, as well as holding down a part-time job. That woman deserved a medal. I know that I couldn't have done what she was doing because Sharon had very challenging behaviour. It was easy to see why. She had been treated very cruelly, and had been taken away from her birth mother when she was four years old. However, the damage had been done, and it was going to take a lot of patience and love to turn her life around.

I don't know why I took Sharon on really. By this time I was teaching SEN children on a permanent contract in one mainstream school, and was quite content there. Sharon's reputation had gone before her so that I knew how difficult she could be. I didn't know the school at all and only knew one teacher there, who happened to be Sharon's teacher. But, there was the point that I like a challenge and somebody had to teach her, didn't they?

Because Sharon was going to be found a place in a unit for children with behaviour problems, I knew that this could just be a term's work and that suited me fine, especially after our first meeting!

I walked into Sharon's classroom that first occasion with a positive attitude, but felt a little nervous when her teacher had to chase her round the room and 'capture' her.

Fortunately we were going to work in the classroom

next door, so I managed to persuade her that she really wanted to go in there, and with the promise of a look in my toy bag, she acquiesced. She wouldn't hold my hand though, and I soon realized that I was going to need a lot of energy to keep up with Sharon as she charged on ahead of me.

She was a very small child for her age, the result of her having had a very inadequate diet. In fact, I knew that she had been found looking for scraps of food in neighbours' dustbins when she had been living with her alcoholic mother.

Her hair was a mousy brown colour cut into a rather plain 'pudding basin' bob. It did nothing for her, especially as she had a rather plain face to go with it. Her expression was one of world weariness, very understandable when you heard about her background, but very worrying in such a young child. This expression never changed, and it was many months before we saw the tiniest of smiles appear on her face, which looked much older than her peers' faces.

She was wearing a pretty summer dress and she constantly smoothed it down or fiddled with the buttons or the bows on it. She'd never had pretty clothes before and the novelty still hadn't worn off.

She sat down next to me and I produced some very simple games, and started to talk to her to get to know her. She stared at the games, but made no attempt to interact with me or to have eye contact. I wittered on with a feeling of panic rising in me. I surreptitiously looked at my watch after what I thought was a good ten minutes, and saw to my dismay that only two minutes had elapsed.

Sharon looked away and started to examine the contents of the room, and I knew that I had 'lost' her. There was a display of objects and pictures that another teacher had set up in one corner of the room and she set off towards it. I leapt up and heard myself say, "Yes, Sharon, that's a good idea, let's look at these toys, shall we?"

She totally ignored me and started to destroy the whole display. Objects went flying through the air and the more fragile things were broken. I tried cajoling her, I tried using a stern voice, but I had ceased to exist as far as Sharon was concerned, and whatever she wanted to do, she was going to do it.

I felt totally helpless and powerless, and the reality was that I was being defeated by a six year old girl. I'd had bad starts before with children, but this really took the biscuit. However was I going to get her back to the classroom? Was it professional to give up after just one session?

I resorted to producing my toy bag rather early in the session and, after I had tipped out the entire contents onto the table and pretended to play with the toys, she eventually wandered over, curiosity getting the better of her. She showed some interest in a spinning top, and before that interest waned and I 'lost' her again, I packed everything away with the promise of playing with it again at the next session. Always leave them wanting more!

Apparently I looked rather grey when I took her back to her classroom, and I was rather subdued that evening. My husband was very concerned, insisting that I could give up now but, remembering Peter and his awful behaviour on our first session, I decided to carry on. I couldn't give up on her so early because she had been let down by many other adults, and I didn't want to join the list. Besides, there was something appealing about her, but I knew that I was going to have to change my game plan - and soon!

My planning for Sharon's sessions had been based on the fact that I was going to try to teach her some basic pre-literacy, pre-number skills. That would include how to write her name etc.

I soon abandoned that plan. She just wasn't ready for anything like work, however informal and basic, and I decided that, as she was in such emotional turmoil and, in mental development was like a toddler, my main aims were to make her happier, interested in her school environment, and to give her teacher a break for two hours a week. I included her fellow class mates in the latter as she could be quite aggressive towards them, too.

So, the next week I took with me my old teddy bear called Marmaduke, and borrowed a couple of soft toys from the classroom.

I would have loved to have taught Sharon some cooking skills, but it was too risky a proposition, so I bought some plain buns and took in some icing sugar, cocoa, chocolate buttons and Smarties. I hoped that a blunt school dinner knife would not pose a threat to either of us, and it is hard to spread icing without a knife! My aim was for us to decorate the buns and then to have a tea-party with the soft toys, hopefully sharing the buns later with her teacher and other adults in the school.

Sharon's interest in Marmaduke was very moving to see. She visibly brightened up and relaxed when she was allowed to cuddle him, although my beady eyes were on her all the time. Her speech was immature, very limited in vocabulary, and sometimes hard to understand, but she managed to learn to say Marmaduke's name, after much practice, and was very pleased with herself.

The sight of the buns was the only thing that would make her put Marmaduke down, and she was so obviously pleased at the thought of eating them later. I was feeling quite positive, until I braced myself for the mixing of the icing. Well, if you haven't managed to persuade a hyper-active, emotionally damaged, toddler-like child, to put only a few drops of water into the icing sugar, then you haven't known what tension is!

Anyway, we eventually had it all mixed and started to spread it onto the buns. I hadn't realized just how many ways of doing that there were, and how grate-ful I was that I had put protective covering on the table and on the floor!

It reminded me of the time that I was working in a Nursery and was sitting talking to a little boy with a bowl of icing sugar and cocoa powder in front of him, as we waited for the buns that we were going to decorate to cool. Suddenly he sneezed right into the bowl and when he lifted his head he had a little brown face! He was rather shocked so I couldn't laugh out loud in front of him, and I had to work hard to stifle my giggles! You'll be pleased to hear that we threw the icing sugar away and started again!

We sat the toys on the floor on a rug I had brought in and Sharon soon entered into the spirit of the thing as I taught her how to offer a bun to someone and what to say. She picked that up quickly and really seemed to be enjoying herself.

"You have a bun?" she would enquire of each toy in turn.

I let her eat three buns herself, working on the premise that if she was feeling full, and this was just after the lunch break, she would be willing to share the rest. To my relief, she was happy to do so, and we both proudly went to the Secretaries, the Headteacher and her Class Teacher to offer them a bun.

"You have a bun?" she enquired again, much to the amazement of everyone, but all said that they would save one for their coffee break later! Cowards!

However, they made a considerable fuss of her, and said all the right things, so that she came away looking reasonably pleased with herself. That's one thing that I was always sure of in all the schools where I worked. All the Staff, whether they were Caretakers, Secretaries, Headteachers, Teaching Assistants or Teachers would always be very positive with the children with SEN, and would back me up in all my, sometimes unusual, endeavours.

Sharon was reluctant to say goodbye to Marmaduke, but was reassured that he would come the next day, so she gave him back to me. If only I had realised the implications of this, I would have never brought him in again, but that's another story.

I never knew how Sharon was going to be from one session to the next. Some days she would seem to be quite calm, although that could all change at any moment; while other days she would be in a bad mood, and my heart would sink as I realised that she was going to be more of a problem than usual.

Snails, Woodlice and Butterflies

The trouble with Sharon was that I never knew what she was going to do next. She had this restless energy which I was always trying to harness and contain. Trying to get her to sit down was the first hurdle, then getting her to stay in the same room as me without wrecking it, then containing her within the school buildings, and finally stopping her from leaving the school grounds.

Every lesson was a very tense time and my levels of adrenaline must have been horrific. Each session required meticulous planning, but this would often have to be abandoned as I struggled to keep her in check. Poor Sharon - I often wondered what was going on in her head and, knowing that she had been the victim of cruelty, I carried on trying to bring some pleasure into her life.

We did the tea party fairly often at her request, but I searched around for something else which would hold her interest. Then, one day, I arrived at school just as her class was coming in from playtime. The Class Teacher was looking rather harassed as Sharon, as was her wont, had refused to line up with her class and was hiding behind a tree, much to the amusement of the other children.

I dumped my bag on the ground and prepared to do my impression of a sheepdog and try to round her up. I didn't want an audience though, so with a huge sigh of relief, her teacher took the other children inside. Yet again, I was seen as the cavalry!

I girded my loins, metaphorically speaking, and tried to work out my plan. I don't know why because plans never worked with Sharon, but hey, it was worth a try.

I pretended to ignore her, while at the same time checking where she was and how far away she was from the school gate. Fortunately I didn't have high heels on that day so was reasonably confident about giving chase!

She skipped from one tree to another in her attempt to get me to chase her. She would have loved that but it was a trap that I wasn't going to fall into if I could help it. I bent down to look at one of the flowers in a border, all the while keeping an eye on her. Oh heck, where had she gone?

I couldn't see her and a feeling of panic engulfed me. A quick look at the gate reassured me. It was firmly shut, and if she had gone through it she wouldn't have stopped to fasten it, particularly as it wasn't the easiest of catches.

I tiptoed up to the tree where I had last seen her, and was relieved to spot the blue of her skirt on the grass. Mind you, I wouldn't have been surprised to find that she had taken it off and run away, just to fool me! She was sitting there, totally engrossed in watching a butterfly that had settled on a twig right in front of her. Oh, thank you, butterfly!

I sat down beside her and she made no attempt to move. I wasn't sure whether she even knew what it was, so I whispered, "What a pretty butterfly!"

"B'fly," she attempted to say in a voice that was too loud for the insect which promptly flew away.

"B'fly," she wailed. "B'fly."

I took her hand and helped her to her feet.

"Come on, let's go and look for more insects! Maybe we'll see some more butterflies!"

All thoughts of doing any formal work went out of

the window completely as we walked round the garden looking for anything that moved. Thank goodness it was Summer and there were plenty of butterflies around. We even found a ladybird, although Sharon shied away as soon as it started to crawl along the leaf towards her. She clutched my arm in panic, but relaxed a little as I steered it away from her. We sat for ages watching the colourful insect dashing around, while Sharon stared at it in wonder.

A woodlouse scurrying along made her jump with fright and, again, she clung onto me as if terrified of it, but then, after a few minutes she couldn't tear herself away from it. I was amazed, and grateful, that all these little creatures could hold her attention. All the time my mind was working overtime, as I worked out how to harness this hitherto undiscovered interest in nature.

She smelt the roses, nearly falling in the flowerbed as she did so, and I was overjoyed to hear a, "Mm!" of delight coming from her.

I was amazed to see from my watch that I should have taken her back to the class five minutes ago, and all thoughts of being punctual for my next pupil in my next school went right out of the window. This moment was too precious to end abruptly. However, the sudden explosion of sound as a class of ten and eleven year olds came out to do PE in the fresh air, brought us back to reality and we ambled back into the classroom.

Her teacher looked gratefully at me. She had had a really good lesson with the rest of the class, and although I had brought Sharon back, at least she was in a better mood.

I walked out of the school that day with my mind buzzing as I contemplated the implications of that day's revelations. What a breakthrough!

The next day in my garden I picked up another pesky snail and prepared to dispatch him to a better place, when I was suddenly reminded of a project I had done many years ago with Infant children all about snails. There was a lot of Literacy, Numeracy, Science and Art work to be found studying these creatures, and we had a lot of fun having snail races! So I rounded up a few and took them in for the next day's session with Sharon.

She was in a good mood that day, and was very interested to know what was in the box I had brought. I carefully took the lid off and she peered in eagerly. She looked rather disdainful as she spotted the snail shell with the snail tucked up safely inside it. Well, if Sharon had been peering at me like that I would have done the same!

I picked up the snail quickly before she had time to lose interest, and was gratified to see the snail begin to emerge from its shell. Sharon's arm clutched mine in a vice-like grip, but her eyes never left the snail and she stayed in her seat.

I put the snail down gently on a piece of clear plastic and we sat there watching it, with me talking gently to Sharon about what the snail was doing, what he ate etc. Gradually, she seemed to lose her fear and slowly but surely she loosened her grip on my arm. She peered again into the box, aware that there was another one in there, and eventually she picked it up, much to my amazement. Now that was progress!

Snails, Woodlice and Butterflies

I suppose that some people might think that it was a rather unusual idea to take snails in for a little girl but I don't like to stereotype children, and Sharon was not a usual child. Oh, and I was getting desperate!

The next day I brought the snails in again, and watched with some satisfaction as Sharon slowly began to show some interest and held one herself again. I had brought the piece of plastic sheet again (not a sheet of glass as that would have been too risky!) and we watched fascinated from underneath, as the snail chewed a leaf. We then had a snail race, although that wasn't a huge success, but nevertheless it kept Sharon occupied for the session.

A good friend of mine, aware of Sharon's interest in insects and creepy crawlies, made me a plastic box, full of grass, soil, leaves and insects and we spent time investigating this. As with anything that I took in for Sharon, the shelf life was limited, and I soon realised that I would have to find another avenue for her energy and interest.

The only exception was Marmaduke, the teddy bear, which Sharon absolutely idolised. She cuddled him most of the time and was reluctant to let him go at the end of each session. Her obsession should have rung alarm bells, but I think I was just grateful that she took pleasure from him.

The school had a wildlife area at the far end of the school grounds and I went to investigate whether it would be a good teaching resource for Sharon. There was a pond - hmm, too risky perhaps? - ducks, and lots of logs which when turned over revealed a rich source of interest. I decided to risk it.

It was difficult to get right to the edge of the pond

so I wasn't worried so much about her falling in. Her behaviour wasn't too bad at the moment, but I did worry about how we were going to get there, bearing in mind her tendency to run off. Even if we were heading in the same direction with the same goal, I wanted to keep her near to me at all times.

So, I collected her from her classroom and told her where we were going. She looked really thrilled and eagerly started to pull away from my hand. I was ready for this.

"When we get to the field we'll run together, OK?" I said firmly. Sharon looked at me in amazement and with a bemused look in her eyes - a teacher, run? I don't think she believed that somebody as ancient as me could possibly run!

Yes, well, it was going to take some believing on my part as well, but we walked round the school, then, with Sharon leading the way, and holding hands, we set off to run a marathon - well, that's what it felt like to me! With my lungs bursting and a stitch in my side, we finally reached the gate and went in, with me firmly locking it behind us. Sharon, needless to say, was hardly out of breath!

We stood by the pond and as soon as a duck appeared Sharon clutched my arm and looked terrified. We had this same pattern of behaviour every time we encountered some new species of wildlife, but every time she would eventually lose her fear and become fascinated. I, too, saw things through a child's eyes and became quite fascinated myself.

We spent sessions just sitting on the grass, watching wood lice, our favourites, scurrying along, negotiating obstacles that Sharon would place in their way.

Of course, with a class of children there would have been opportunities for Writing, Science, Art activities etc to take place back in the classroom but that was not possible with Sharon, and I accepted that written proof of our expeditions would never exist. OFSTED Inspectors would have hated that!

If they had ever questioned what I was doing with Sharon (and the teachers, Headteacher and my boss never did), I would quite happily have invited them to spend a session with her on their own. That would have shut them up!

§

I was always nattering the SENCo to see whether she knew what was going to happen to Sharon and when, or if, she would be moving on to the Behaviour Unit. The truth was that I knew I couldn't carry on much longer with her.

My headaches, which had improved in recent years, were becoming more frequent, and I approached each session with great trepidation, wondering whether I would be able to interest her enough to keep control of her. The Headteacher and Class Teacher were great and kept saying that I was doing a good job, and that Sharon liked me, but that was not enough. I began counting off the sessions until the end of term. Then, more quickly than I would have dreamt, we were into the last week of term.

I was always honest with the children in my care, and told them what was going to happen in the case of any major changes. So, with a week to go, I told Sharon that next term I wouldn't be coming any more as she would be in a new class and things would be different and… I tailed off as a look of panic and horror came over her face.

"What about Marmaduke?" she asked forlornly.

"No," I said firmly, "Marmaduke will stay at home with me."

Sharon's reaction was so extreme and so unexpected that it completely caught me off guard. She put her head down on the table and sobbed as if her heart was broken. And it was me who had broken it. I felt such pity and sorrow for this sad little girl who had led me a merry dance, but I had become very fond of her and I hated to see her like this.

I then did something that I had never done before and, to my horror, I felt tears coursing down my cheeks. I had never cried in front of a child, although I had sometimes felt like it, and I heard myself say, "Oh, Sharon, don't!"

She raised her head then and stared at me, not in anger but in real distress. I hastily composed myself and thought quickly. There was no way that I could give Marmaduke away to Sharon, as he was of great sentimental value to me and my husband, but maybe there was something else I could do…

"Sharon, how about if Marmaduke has a friend who would come and stay with you?"

She nodded weakly and, through her tears she managed to say, "Another teddy?"

"Yes, another teddy who would be all yours, and who would stay with you forever."

She seemed to be reassured by this, and by the time that I took her back to her classroom she was more composed.

My husband and I spent the next few days going round all the toy and gift shops looking for a teddy bear which looked like Marmaduke! We eventually found a pretty good lookalike, and I wrapped him up and took him in for Sharon. She loved him, but still cried when she had to say goodbye to Marmaduke, and to me.

When I took her back to her classroom for the last time, it was dinner time and she went off with one of the dinner ladies. I looked at her teacher, a lady I had known for years, and started to fill up.

"She will be alright, won't she? I feel that I'm just abandoning her!"

"Yes, of course," she reassured me, "Sharon is a survivor!"

She was right, of course, and whenever I saw people from the school in the following years, they made a point of telling me that she was doing well. In fact, she never did transfer to a Behaviour Unit, as it was felt that she was beginning to settle down and, with her home life more stable now, she remained in her mainstream school.

It is a tribute to all the Staff that they managed to keep her with them, and so spared her yet another change. With this new stability in her life, she settled down and became a much happier girl. I'll never forget her.

9

Look Out, Paula Radcliffe!

Wayne had Severe Learning Difficulties and - here we go again - behaviour problems. It would have been difficult for me to have refused to teach him, as I was already working in that school, so I started off in my usual optimistic way, and to start with he was fine. We always said that there was a honeymoon period in any new relationship with a child! He trotted down the corridor, being very co-operative, although my cheerful conversation only elicited monosyllabic grunts.

He was tall for his age - he was eight years old - and he had a shock of blonde hair with the freckles to match. He had three brothers in the same school and they were all a bit of a handful, although the phrase 'loveable rogues' comes to mind, as none of them was really bad.

The great thing about Wayne, and the unusual thing too, was that he loved number games, so the reward of being able to choose one from my store at the end of the lesson, when he had done some work, usually worked a treat.

He would choose the same game every time and I thought I would go out of my mind with boredom. Occasionally he would choose a different one, but would always revert to his favourite. Ah well, as a ~~bribe~~, sorry, reward, it was brilliant.

After a while, the novelty of having a new teacher wore off, and his behaviour started to deteriorate. He knew how to wind us all up, but it was so easy to reward him by dangling the metaphorical carrot that his antics really amused me.

He would refuse to co-operate, or would say silly answers, but would produce the correct answer when reminded that it was nearly playtime, and did he want to go out to play, or I produced my toy bag or pointed at my collection of games.

I used to sit in my room, waiting for him to appear at the appropriate time, after lunch. This was not the way I usually worked. The teachers were far too busy to have to remember to send the children to me, so I always collected them from the classroom. At one of his review meetings, it was deemed that as one of Wayne's targets, he should come under his own steam. However, Wayne's natural resistance to doing what we all wanted, and his interest in anything that was not his business, meant that I could be sitting twiddling my thumbs while a one-minute journey took Wayne the best part of ten minutes. There was always the worry that he would decide to go out of the school building, and then who knew where he would end up?

So, I used to end up going to meet him and then pretending that we had met by accident!

The conversation would consist of me saying, "Oh, Wayne, fancy meeting you here! You're just the person I wanted to see!"

At first I think that he was fooled, but when I had to search the toilets for him, my story looked a bit thin! (That shows how desperate I was to find him, as no adult went into the boys' toilets without a gas mask on!)

It's a known fact that children with Special Needs are often to be found in the toilets. It's nothing to do with them having weak bladders, but rather it is a response to the pressure that they feel in the classroom, trying to keep up with the other children.

They are also often to be found near the bin in the classroom, as they very, very slowly sharpen their pencils. When they have taken a few cms off the original length and the bin is full of shavings, and the teacher has cottoned on to what they are doing, they reluctantly go back to their seats, only to realise that they need to search the floor intently for their eraser/ paper/ruler etc.

If, while they are on the floor, they can cause havoc by interfering with the other children, well, it all adds to the fun!

This particular day, I was aghast when one of his classmates came down to my room and announced,

"Wayne is sitting crying and the teacher says will you come and get him, please?"

Was I really such an ogre? I didn't really think so and it was soon obvious that this was another of Wayne's ploys to get out of work. So, I accompanied the child down to the classroom to go and rescue the teacher and the class. Boy, could Wayne howl! We realised later that he had seen another child become distressed and cry (for a very good reason), and they had been taken out of the classroom and missed the lesson, and he had stored it up in his memory!

Usually I could cajole him, or offer some sort of reward to induce him to come with me, but that day, nothing would work.

I was feeling a bit desperate, especially as the whole class of eight and nine year olds were watching things with interest, and wondering what on earth I was going to do next. I was wondering the same thing, I must admit! There was no way that the teacher could teach with that noise going on, so I'm afraid that I succumbed to desperate measures.

I very rarely gave children sweets for doing well but, hey, I was fresh out of other ideas and, knowing how Wayne loved his food, especially the sweet variety, I bent down and whispered in his ear, "I've got a lollipop in my room!"

I did keep a store of sweets for special occasions so I was telling the truth!

Blow me, he instantly stopped crying, smiled and said, "Come on then, let's go!" He shot out of the room with me trying to keep up with him. The funny thing was that by the time we had got to my room and I started to show him other interesting things, he had forgotten all about the lollipop!

Later on, when I was working in my room at break time, there was a knock on the door and two of Wayne's classmates came in. They had obviously witnessed Wayne's tantrum and rapid capitulation.

"Do you mind if we ask you something, Mrs Young?"

"No, as long as you don't mind if I can't give you an answer," I said, covering myself.

"We just wondered what you said to Wayne to get him to go with you."

"Ah!" I replied, trying to look mysterious. "I'm afraid that I can't divulge one of my special techniques." They looked disappointed but had the grace not to natter me!

§

The children I taught were often full of surprises

and Wayne was no exception. I thought that I knew him really well and could anticipate what he would do. How wrong can you be!

One day, his Mum was having trouble getting him to come into the school and, as I happened to be on the spot, I was asked to come and help. This was quite an unusual situation and it surprised me to see him so defiant with his Mum. He was standing near the front door, fortunately on the inside, glowering at every-body within sight.

Oh good, I thought, it's not even nine o'clock and we've got problems!

His Mum was standing by the Office door, a few yards away, looking harassed and cross.

"Wayne, get yourself down to your classroom this minute or I'll give you what for!"

It is never a good idea to get into a confrontational situation with a child. They have nowhere to go, and can't back down, so dig their heels in even more. If you give them a choice and try to defuse the situation then you are more likely to achieve a reasonably good result. Well, that's the theory, anyway!

"You wait 'til you come home tonight and your Dad hears about this!"

As his Mum threatened him and shouted at him, Wayne became more determined to remain where he was, just near the door out into the front of the school. Now, when I point out that the school was just a few feet away from a main road, which Wayne had to cross to get to his house, you may wonder at the wisdom of my next comments. In my defence, I had to get him away from his Mum, and he had never done a runner before.

Look Out, Paula Radcliffe!

I tried to usher his Mum into the Office and when her eyes flickered over towards the door, I read her mind and said very quietly, "Don't worry, he won't open the door and go out. Let's just give him time to cool down."

I had intended to stroll towards him, engage him in conversation and slowly bring him round. However, as soon as I had uttered this rather inaccurate statement, we heard the front door open and slam.

I peered round the Office door and was horrified to see that he had indeed done a runner!

In a split second I flew out of the Office, out of the door and down the street after him! I had never moved so fast in my life, and this was all the more surprising as I was wearing high heels that day!

I had this vision of Wayne swerving across the road to get to his house right in front of a lorry which couldn't stop and... it's amazing what a rush of adrenaline can do for you. I had heard about people who could lift a car up in a dire emergency and, while running and wearing high heels and having asthma combined was not as heroic and extreme, it was certainly out of character.

Somehow, I was gaining on him and as he looked round I was only a yard or so away.

If only he would run round the corner, into the cul-de-sac and away from the main road I could maybe corner him, or at least keep my eye on him until reinforcements arrived.

My prayers were answered, and he did indeed go into the cul-de-sac, slowing down considerably. Of course, by this time the enormity of the situation had hit him and he wanted to be caught and taken back to school. This was unfamiliar territory and he was very unsure of himself.

He leaned against a garden wall, as out of breath as I was (well nearly), and bent over, pretending to be very interested in a leaf that happened to float down in front of him.

I slowly walked up to him.

"By, Wayne, you can run fast. I think that you'll do well on Sports Day if you run like that in the races. If you did some training as well…" Yes, I was in witter mode again but it seemed to be working.

A sheepish grin came over his face.

"Cor, Miss Young, you can run fast an' all. I got a right shock when I looked round an' you were right behind me."

I smiled. "Yeah, not bad for an old fogey, eh?"

There was a pause. "Come on, let's go and have a drink and a biscuit in my room. I think I've deserved it, don't you?"

This time I had said just the right thing and we walked calmly back up the road and into school.

The Secretary was hovering nearby as we entered, and I smiled reassuringly at her.

"Everything is fine," I said. "I'll see you later."

I took Wayne to my room while she persuaded Mum to go home, having seen that Wayne was safe.

Later on, when I had recovered, I strolled into the Office and asked the question that had been bothering me.

"I don't suppose that anyone thought to come after me, you know, as back up?"

"You're joking, Pam, aren't you? You were going so fast that none of us here could have kept up. It really was a most impressive display, especially in those heels!"

The longer that I taught Wayne, the more rewards I had to come up with. As I said, he loved his food and I toyed with the idea of cooking lessons, but his behaviour was so erratic that I hesitated. However, the day came when I had run out of other ideas, so we started simply with icing buns, using bought buns. One thing at a time! If there are lots of different things to put on the buns then the child's creative side can be brought out.

Now, if I thought that Dennis could write a book on 'One Hundred And One Ways To Break An Egg And Still Miss The Bowl', then Wayne could have made Dennis look like a master Chef! He always thought that he knew best and, although I might think I was in charge, he knew that it was really him, and he was determined to do everything his way!

I insisted on pouring the water into the icing sugar and thank goodness I had put paper all over the table. We didn't quite have icing hanging from the lights, but it was a close run thing! He was so determined and I let him have his own way when it came to decorating the buns with Smarties, Hundreds and Thousands, cherries etc.

I let him eat one bun, then he asked for another, then another. He would have eaten all twelve buns if I had let him! I persuaded him to share some with the Staff and he took some home for his family. He was very reluctant to wash up but when asked the question, "Do you want to bake again?" he took the hint. The bubbles in the washing up bowl helped as well!

We gradually moved on to 'proper' cooking and our

efforts became more and more ambitious. It was such hard work for me though. He was very impetuous, and could grab something so quickly that I needed to be on my guard all the time. If we needed the oven to be on, I would surround it with chairs so that he couldn't get to it. (The oven couldn't be anywhere else because it was my responsibility and so I had to be able to see it.)

Sharp knives were out of the question of course, so sometimes we had to hack at things with a rather blunt one. If he needed to pour liquid into another container, I would move it very swiftly to try to catch the liquid, as his movements were rather jerky and he couldn't always aim straight.

When stirring the ingredients for a cake, he would rapidly disappear behind a cloud of flour as everything went flying up to land, hopefully on the (clean) paper that covered the table, so that I could scoop it back into the bowl. Bless him, he did see the funny side of it and was very tolerant of my efforts to help him.

Chocolate was his favourite ingredient and I can picture him now with a spoon and bowl, licking out the bowl when we had finished. He had chocolate all round his mouth and a grin from ear to ear!

Some time later, *Teacher* magazine ran a photography competition and the subject was 'What Makes The Job Worthwhile.' My husband suggested that I take a photo of my payslip and submit that, but I somehow didn't think that was quite what they meant! I wished I had taken a photo of Wayne, as I have just described him, because I feel sure we would have had a very good chance of winning, and he would have loved the glory.

Back to the cooking, which was his favourite thing. Quite often, as we cooked, we would be aware that a little boy from the next door Reception class, who also had Severe Learning Difficulties and other problems including communication problems, would be watching us through the window in my door with his Pupil Support Assistant, Mary, as we whipped up another culinary masterpiece. The look of envy on his face haunted me for quite a while, until I approached Mary and said to her, "What do you think about Henry cooking with us, as long as you come too?"

"I thought you'd never ask!" she declared. "I've been hoping that you would see how much he wants to join you, and I think he would get a lot out of it."

So began some of the most frantic and stressful Cookery lessons on the planet! You would think that just two children with two adults was the right ratio and it would be easy. Wrong!

Both children were very quick to seize something for nefarious purposes or just out of curiosity, and we both spent the sessions trying to be one step ahead of them by guessing what they were going to grab next. After they had gone we would sit in a heap with mugs of coffee as we tried to restore our senses.

However, it was usually worth it, because Wayne came into his own and showed us the lovely side of his nature. He was like a father to Henry, tenderly helping him and showing him what to do next, and being amazingly patient when he was unsure or messed things up. If he dropped something on the floor, he cleared it up for him, saying, "Never mind, it doesn't matter," when Henry looked aghast.

Did he recognize that they were alike, but Henry had additional problems, and so was more needy than he was? For once in his life, did he think that he was the more able child? The situation must have been quite empowering for him. No wonder he was always asking when Henry was coming next.

Unusually, Henry wasn't quite so keen on sweet stuff as Wayne, although when we cooked with chocolate they both loved to see how much of the melted stuff they could get on their faces! But the day came when Henry lost interest and didn't want to come anymore. Wayne couldn't understand this at all. What, pass up the chance to eat buns and chocolate and cake? What was he thinking of?

We continued as before, but it was never quite the same, although I had to admit it was very much easier without Henry, much as I liked him and admired the progress he was making.

I tried, in vain, to encourage Wayne to cook something savoury, but he had no interest in that at all. He did learn to share what we made more willingly, though, and he could be trusted to take cakes home for his family.

10

Did I Really Say That?

Shane came very reluctantly out of the classroom when I went to collect him for our first session. I knew that he had Dyslexia and that his behaviour was becoming a problem in the classroom and play-ground, and I also soon realised that on a scale of one to ten, his self-esteem was minus ten.

He was very tall for his age, and it was easy to see that his size and his manner could appear threatening to much smaller children in the playground. His dark hair flopped in his eyes and over the back of his collar. His school sweatshirt was frayed at the cuffs, where he had been chewing at them, in boredom and frustration. I could always tell what he had eaten for breakfast and school dinner, as there were little bits of food all down his shirt, some encrusted with age. It didn't look as though it had ever been washed. There were also tell tale marks round his mouth and later, when I got to know him better, I would astound him by telling him what he had had for lunch when I had just arrived at two o'clock.

"Cor, that's magic, Miss Young," he would shout. "How d'yer know?"

"Oh, it's just a lucky guess," I would say with an innocent look on my face. It worked every time.

He had a permanent scowl on **his** face, I had been told, and he was never seen to smile. Hmm, we'll soon see about that, I thought optimistically.

We sat down in my room and he looked furtively around, as if he expected me to produce lots of work which he could then refuse to do, and so maintain his reputation as a very difficult child. After a brief survey he settled on examining the floor.

"So," I began, "did you see Man United's match last night on TV?"

I had done my homework and knew that the one thing that he enjoyed in life was football.

His head jerked up in surprise.

He nodded but still refused to take the trouble to speak to me.

"Wayne Rooney's goal was a good one, wasn't it?"

I had surprised him again. Little did he know that I had questioned the only male member of Staff at break time about the match, so that I was well prepared.

"Yeah!" he answered, despite himself.

Meanwhile I was over the moon that I had managed to get a civil word out of him. OK, it was literally only one word, but it was a start.

We had soon exhausted my knowledge of last night's game and, although I realised that a discussion of the offside rule might impress him even more, I knew my limitations. I had realised early in my career though, that an interest in football would be an advantage, and so it had proved time and time again.

I asked him about his family, his favourite food, and what he liked to watch on television. The answers were mostly monosyllabic. Well, let's be honest, they all were, but at least he hadn't thrown a 'wobbly', and to my surprise I found that we only had five minutes of our session together left.

Now, in my job you often had to take risks. They were mostly calculated risks but nevertheless, they were risks.

I decided to take one now.

"Before you go out to play, Shane, you need to do one thing for me."

He groaned, obviously thinking that I was going to ask him to do some work, or something which, in his mind, he wouldn't be able to do.

I had to hold my nerve. This could either improve our relationship or set it back to the beginning.

"No, don't worry, all I need you to do is to think of one thing that you're good at."

A look of bewilderment came over his face. Is this woman mad? I'm not good at anything, am I?

I took another risk. "I'll let you go out to play when you've told me one thing. I don't mind whether it's eating spaghetti noisily, or sucking gobstoppers for a long time, but I need to know one thing. Then you can go."

Of course I was running the risk that he would just get up and flounce out anyway, but I thought that it was worth a try.

The slightest flicker of a smile appeared briefly on his face. Or had I imagined it?

"Football," I heard him say, much to my delight.

"Well done," I enthused. "That's what I had heard. Right, off you go and I'll see you tomorrow. OK?"

I hadn't really expected an answer, but as he jumped up and headed towards the door I thought that I heard a little voice say, "OK!"

I couldn't be sure, you understand but, hopefully, I had.

The next day I collected him straight after lunch time. This time is never a good one for pupils like Shane, as the playground is a minefield with a great potential for getting into trouble.

They never, ever, saw any problems as their fault, so they often came to me resentful and aggressive with attitude written all over their faces.

They would often take it out on me, and I had had nothing to do with the situation!

If they had been running around playing football they were often puffed out and rather sweaty, especially in the Summer. I never relished sitting next to an eleven year old boy who had been exerting himself a lot.

Shane sniffed and adopted a suitable sneer as he came to me, taking his time as if he were in charge. That was another problem with my pupils (yes, yet another one). They often felt powerless and out of control so they would do anything they could to try to tip the balance of power in their favour, if not seize it altogether.

We eventually made it to my room, with me chattering away about anything and everything.

As we sat down and he looked furtively around, I said, "You thought of one thing yesterday that you were good at, and that was playing football, wasn't it?"

He nodded.

"Well, today you have to think of another thing, then that will make two things!"

Oh, this mad woman!

Then he grinned. "I'm good at sleeping in on a morning. My Mum has a right job getting me out of bed!"

Well, it wasn't quite what I had in mind but it would do.

The third day he knew what was coming.

"I can burp really loudly, especially when I've eaten pickled onions, and when I eat baked beans you should hear me…"

"Thank you, Shane!" I interjected swiftly. "Burping will be fine!"

Oh, what was I saying? Put into context it doesn't sound too bad, but taken on its own it wasn't quite what I meant to say! However, that was the longest sentence that he had uttered, and I felt rather pleased. It didn't take much!

The fourth day I thought that we had hit a brick wall as he struggled to think of yet another thing that he was good at.

"I'm good at making paper aeroplanes," he grudgingly admitted.

On the fifth day he had anticipated his task and had sought help from his Dad.

"My Dad says that I'm good at banging in nails!"

I visibly winced, then quickly recovered myself. You mean that someone actually entrusts a hammer and nail to you, I thought.

It was more than I would do.

But, after five sessions, he had thought of five things that he was good at, and his self-esteem had greatly increased. Result!

§

One of Shane's little foibles was that he would swear under his breath at anybody that he was working with. The word, usually 'bastard', was just audible, so that the first time that he uttered it in my hearing, I was quite taken aback and wondered if I had heard him correctly. Two minutes later I was sure.

"I heard that, Shane," I said sternly. "Don't use that word again, please."

He looked at me in mock amazement.

"What?" he said in his gruff voice, looking as if the proverbial butter wouldn't melt in his mouth.

"You know what," I persisted.

"Hmm," was the best that he could come up with at that moment, and I tried to distract him with another activity.

Five minutes later, he made the mistake of uttering the word again.

"Bastard!" came sotto voce, but not sotto voce enough. He had the grace to look slightly ashamed of himself, and looked very contrite when I declared, "Right, that's enough. You won't be getting a sticker today, and if I hear that word again I shall ask Mr Smith to ban you from the next football session."

He knew when he was beaten, and I never heard the word again.

One day he came to me in a really foul mood, and no amount of cajoling could bring him round. I wasn't having a good day myself, so all in all it was on the cards that something had to give.

He suddenly stood up and headed towards the door.

"I'm off and you can stuff your book!"

The door slammed shut and I slumped back in my chair. I really should go and look for him, I thought, but I don't know whether I've got the energy.

Fortunately, professionalism overcame weariness, and I opened the door and peered out.

I nearly jumped out of my skin because there, sitting

on a bench in the adjacent cloakroom, almost directly outside my room, was Shane.

He raised his world-weary face to my own.

"I couldn't think of anywhere to go," he muttered, on seeing the look of surprise on my face.

"I'll tell you what, Shane, I'm having an awful day as well. Come back in and we'll make ourselves badges that say 'Leave me alone. I'm having a bad day!'

I smiled at him.

"And we could play SWAP!" (This was a series of phonics card games that all the children loved to play.) I longed to put my arm round his shoulder but I knew that this would not be appropriate. He looked so disconsolate and vulnerable and my heart ached for him.

He stood up slowly and, to my relief, he came back in. We duly made the badges, but decided that they would be best worn only in my room!

Shane came to love my badges and stickers, and he avidly collected them, as they came in sets. He could take ages to choose one, but as I only gave them out at the end of a session, I didn't mind. They boosted his self-esteem and that was such a valuable thing.

I can only think of one child who didn't value the stickers that I carried with me at all times to reward the children for good work and effort. Even the eleven year old boys used to love to collect them, and I would let them choose where they could display them, usually on their sweatshirts or jumpers, so that everyone could see them.

Their teachers and peers made a point of admiring them and asking why they had been given them.

This increased their self-esteem. I often bought ones that had words on them: 'Good work' or 'You're brilliant!' and so the children learnt to read those words incidentally.

Some took them home and put them on their wardrobes or a sticker chart that their parents bought for them, and some left them on their sweatshirts and put them in the washing machine! It was amazing what good a very small piece of paper could do, and the threat of not being awarded one was enough to change a child's behaviour for the better.

Let's hear it for stickers!

11

Setting Fire To £20 Notes!

I was sitting in the staff room at break one day, having a much-needed cup of tea, when the Deputy Head, Bob, who was sitting next to me, sighed and said, "I'm doing the annual anti-smoking talk to Year Six next - can't say I'm looking forward to it."

We all nodded sympathetically. In June, which is when this conversation occurred, Year Six (ten and eleven year olds) are notorious for their attitude and behaviour in many schools. They have done their SATs (Assessment Tests) in May, and see no point in doing any work as they will soon be leaving for pastures new.

The teachers ran themselves ragged trying to think of new ways to keep them on board for just a few more weeks. This school ran a Health Awareness Project where outside speakers would come in - often with free gifts for them all, so they went down well.

A talk about the dangers of smoking was felt to be worthwhile, although we did wonder if for some of the children it was a case of closing the stable door after the horse had bolted.

At that time my mother-in-law was dying of lung cancer, and it was obviously a very gruelling time for all the family as we watched her struggling for breath and losing her independence.

"I wish that I could take them to see my mother-in-law," I declared vehemently. "That might put a few of them off smoking."

Bob turned and looked me in the eye.

"Well, you could come and talk to them about her and tell them what it's like."

Hmm, me and my big mouth!

"Yes, but, I wouldn't pull any punches, and I wonder if it might be a bit too graphic and frightening…" I tailed off feebly, as we both knew that many of these children were watching videos and computer games every night that would scare the pants off us, but which they just took in their stride.

A mother once admitted to me that her son was watching these evil, depraved films, but said, "What can you do, Mrs Young?"

I wanted to tell her to get a grip and destroy the videos, but as a teacher it is difficult to say these things anymore. It's not politically correct to tell parents what they should do, especially in very firm language, as they are likely to run to the Education Authority to complain about you, or even worse, the local newspaper, which would be fool enough to print their side of the story, knowing full well that we couldn't make any comment on individual cases.

Anyway, I digress.

So, that's how I came to be standing in an empty classroom, waiting for ninety reluctant, lip-curling eleven year olds, who would rather be anywhere else and with anybody else. Bob had assured me there would be plenty of Staff there, and if there was a riot they'd get me out with my life. No, I'm making that last bit up, but that's how it felt! Nervous, me? You bet I was!

Suddenly the door was flung open and they started to swagger in – and that was just the Staff! Just joking! It was a fearsome sight, and the noise itself was enough to make anybody nervous. After all, let's remember that for some years my biggest audience had consisted of four children. I decided that shock tactics were necessary, and as the teachers called the children to order, I decided to go for it.

"My mother-in-law is dying of lung cancer."

I said this very quietly. If I had spoken loudly they wouldn't have had to listen quite so well. The low level buzz of conversation dropped considerably. They were obviously wondering if they had heard me correctly, and if they had, could this be a teeny bit interesting?

"Yes, that's right, my mother-in-law has only a few weeks left to live. She's got lung cancer because she has smoked cigarettes for many years, and although she wanted to give them up, she couldn't. Once they've got you they won't let go and so you become addicted to them. She can hardly talk now, but when she can speak she will often say that she wishes she had never had that first cigarette. Let me tell you what her life is like now."

By now there was total silence, and most of the ninety pairs of eyes were fixed firmly on me. I felt the confidence oozing through me and I went on.

"She used to live for her family, particularly her grandchildren, and she was always taking them out, buying them things, being with them. Now, she knows that she'll never see them again, never hug them, never see them grow up. She'll never see another Christmas or birthday.

She used to love to go on holiday, in this country and abroad. She and her husband have been all over the world and they particularly enjoyed taking the grand-children to Disneyland. Now, she'll never leave the country again. In fact she'll never leave her bedroom again until she's in a box."

I paused, letting that sink in, and wondering if I had gone too far. By now you could have heard a pin drop. "She'll never go out into the country, see the Spring flowers, hear the birds sing, or feel the sunshine on her face. She can't do any of the things she used to enjoy. She can't eat, or chat to people, watch television or read the newspaper. She can't wash herself or even wipe her own bottom."

Again, I wondered if I had gone too far, as usually mentioning the word 'bottom' in a Primary School would cause great merriment and sniggering. Not this time though. The silence was electric and every face had a look of shock on it.

I had been wondering how I was going to finish this talk, and it suddenly came to me.

"She will almost certainly die before our half-term holiday. She is dying a long, slow painful death and all because of that first lousy cigarette."

I then spun on my heel and walked abruptly out of the room.

I must admit that I was shaking and didn't quite know what to do with myself. I wandered slowly up the corridor and then I heard footsteps coming up behind me.

"Pam, are you alright?" enquired Bob, looking very concerned.

"Yes, I think so, but was it OK? Did I go too far?" I needn't have worried.

"It was fantastic!" he said excitedly. "It made a real impact and when I came out to see if you were alright they were still sitting in shocked silence. I haven't seen Year Six so thoughtful for a long time."

"But I wonder if it will have done any good."

"We'll never really know, but if it stops one child from smoking, you will have done some good."

Bless him, he was so positive and so grateful to me, and I would have done it all again for him - in fact I did do the same thing every year - but I'm getting ahead of myself.

During the next few days up to half term, children who I had never spoken to before would stop me in the corridor and ask me how my mother-in-law was. I was very touched by their evident concern.

Then one day, a girl came shyly up to me and said, "I told my Mum all that you said about smoking, and she has stopped smoking now. Thank you."

Jackpot! It had all been worthwhile and I couldn't wait to tell Bob who was as thrilled as I was. Well, nearly, anyway.

My mother-in-law died just after the children had come back to school after the half term holiday. It was decided amongst the Staff that they would get the children together, and that they would tell them the news so that I wouldn't have to do it. Apparently some of the children were quite tearful and upset, and the whole experience had left an impression on them. Many told me later how sorry they were to hear that she had died.

I shall never know if my talk had stopped a child from smoking, or indeed, had persuaded them to give it up. But I'm still proud of my contribution.

A few weeks earlier, when my mother-in-law was still alive, I was working with two of the Year Six pupils, George and Kerry-Anne, who, despite being of the opposite sex, enjoyed each other's company and worked very well together!

We were working our way through a very good reading scheme which had Craft activities and work-sheets to go with it. This particular Craft activity was to make a jewellery box out of card. Yes, well, I could really see George wanting to do that! So, I decided to move onto something else, and produced other work to be done at that session.

George looked up at me thoughtfully and enquired, "Isn't there something to make with this book?"

Kerry-Anne nodded in agreement.

"Yes, well, there was, but it was a jewellery box and I didn't think that you would want to make one of those, George," I tailed off lamely, knowing that I was on a sticky wicket from the looks on their faces.

"But I could have made it for your mother-in-law," declared George, with a reproachful look.

"And I could have made one for you," said Kerry-Anne, making me feel even worse.

I knew when I was beaten.

"Just give me five minutes to find the sheets and photocopy them onto card, and then you can make them," I said contritely.

They made the boxes beautifully. I accepted mine graciously from Kerry-Anne, and George was thrilled when I told him that my mother-in-law had been really touched by his. After she died we found it in her belongings - she hadn't just thrown it away.

That whole experience taught me that you should never anticipate how somebody else will react, but if you do get it wrong, admit it, and put it right as soon as you can. That way you will still have the children's respect.

Setting Fire To £20 Notes!

The Staff decided that the children in Year Five should also hear my talk, and so a few weeks later I did it again, although I felt that it had lost some of its impetus as my mother-in-law had already died.

Every year after that I did the talk but, after time for reflection, I expanded it. Children of that age know the price of everything but the value of nothing, as they are so materialistic. I decided to make them really think, by telling them how much money they would save per week/month/year if they didn't smoke, and what they could buy with that money. Using an overhead projector, I showed them pictures, and they duly looked very interested when I pointed out what they could have. I still talked about the health aspect, but, let's face it, when you're eleven you think that you are immortal.

One of the more impressive parts of the talk was when I got out a £20 note, rolled it up into a cylinder, then got out a box of matches. In total silence, as the children watched in horrified fascination, I put the £20 note to my lips and lit a match, moving it towards my mouth.

As one of the children said to me later, "Cor, Mrs Young, I really thought that you were going to set fire to it!"

As a way of getting the attention of ninety children it is hard to beat!

12

An Inspector Calls

As you will have realised by now, food is a subject close to my heart, and I enjoyed Cookery sessions with the children. But I had often wanted to do more, particularly in influencing what children ate. At many of the schools I taught in, a lot of the children lived on a diet of high-fat and high-sugar foods, and it was obvious that obesity levels would rise. I firmly believed that colourings and additives in junk food could influence children's behaviour too.

I knew that I could only do so much, but anything would be better than nothing, so I decided that I would ask Mr Fox, the Headteacher of Milderton School, where I had most of my pupils, if I could start an after-school Cookery Club. I had a soft spot for this Head anyway, as he had actually had a room made for me in which I could teach my children.

Of course, he was very enthusiastic and told me to go ahead. I approached the teachers of the three Year Six classes in the staff room one day.

"Do you think that any of the children would want to stay after school to come to a Cookery Club?" I asked them.

As most eleven year olds would rather die than stay on after school when they didn't have to, I was dubious as to whether I would get any takers.

"We'll send a notice around the three classes and see if any of them sign up," Bob said.

The next day I approached Bob in the staff room where all three Year Six teachers were sitting.

"Did you have any response to the Cookery Club?" I asked nervously.

The three of them looked at each other and grinned at me.

"What do you think to this then?" smiled Sylvia, and she produced a list of over **eighty** names!

I couldn't believe it and I sank into a chair, not knowing whether to be pleased or daunted.

"I thought that I'd only get a few," I declared. "How am I going to choose from all this lot?"

I had decided that I would have six pupils at a time for six weeks. So, allowing for holidays and other eventualities, I reckoned that I could have two groups every term - in other words, thirty six children per year - and I had over eighty names on the list!

In the end, after discussing the problem, and what a great problem to have, I decided to start with the pupils who had Special Needs, and any who the teachers thought were needy. This included those with behaviour problems, which seemed rather daunting when you have hot pans and sharp knives around, but I thought that I would deal with any problems if, and, when they happened, although I followed all the Health and Safety guidelines, or my common sense, whichever was more appropriate!

The next hurdle to clear was that of who was going to pay for the ingredients. I was used to funding one-off Cookery lessons but I drew the line at all this expense. Mr Fox, the Headteacher, said that some of it could come out of the School Fund but that there wasn't much in it at the moment. Nothing new there then, and the same could be said for every school.

I was an extremely good customer at our local Tesco store so I approached them. They wrote back saying that they couldn't do anything on a regular basis, but they enclosed a voucher for £10. Well, it was a start, and I appreciated their generosity, but I would need more than that. Still, if every supermarket I tried gave me something...

Just as I started to write letters to them all, I saw a picture in the local Press of people who were accepting a donation from the local supermarket where I had often shopped with the children. Well, it was worth a go.

I decided to go down and ask to see the Manager who was duly summoned. I explained what I was hoping to do, and then enquired hopefully, "If you would donate some food to this Cookery Club, we would be very willing to go to the Press and get some good publicity for your store. What do you think?"

A pained expression came over his face. "We would be very willing to provide the food, but we don't crave the publicity. There will be no need to go to the Press."

I felt quite ashamed for suggesting it and could feel myself blushing.

The Manager stuck to his word and every two or three weeks I would go down to the Store, select the items we needed, then go to the Customer Services Desk. The staff there were always so friendly and patient, and the first time that I went they lifted up a huge 'Donations' book from under the counter.

It would appear that I wasn't the only person who benefited from their generosity. Every item in my basket had to be written down, and they never batted an eyelid at how much I had got, although I never took advantage of their generosity, and tried always to be economical.

The next question to be decided was what I was going to cook. I wanted everything to be healthy, but I knew that if I started with raw vegetables and couscous I would lose their interest immediately. So, I decided to cook sweet and savoury items, but realistically I had to start with something sweet.

I chose Chocolate Crunch and Flapjack to begin, followed the next week by Pizza, using a scone base. The next week would be cakes and buns, and the fourth week Spaghetti Bolognese, followed by stuffed jacket potatoes, with biscuits and popcorn for the last week.

If the lessons coincided with a Festival or special day, for example Shrove Tuesday, then we could be flexible and vary the menu accordingly, and if the children came with an idea of something they really wanted to learn to cook, then we could accommodate that too.

After much discussion with their teachers we finally made a list of all the groups of children, and sent a letter to their parents requesting their permission for the children to stay after school. As you can see, it was quite a complicated task setting all this up!

The first Tuesday I staggered into school in the morning with all the ingredients and some of the equipment we would need. Although the school had a well-equipped kitchen for the children, I still liked my own things or had to take in something that wasn't there.

I taught in the morning, then knew that I had all the afternoon to do some lesson preparation and get the Cookery Club set up. I had impressed upon the children that they should be ready to start by half past three, so they must really get a move on and come as soon as they could. I presumed I had thought of everything, but things don't always work out as planned…

At about a quarter to one the School Secretary approached me rather apologetically, and said that one of the teachers had gone home with a migraine and they were having difficulty finding a Supply Teacher. Would I take the class that afternoon? My heart sank as it was the last thing I needed, but they were desperate, so what could I say?

I racked my brain for something to do with the children and we spent the greater part of the afternoon making up acrostics. One of the important things about being a Supply Teacher is that you leave the classroom exactly as you find it.

Many years ago when I was doing a lot of supply work I went into a classroom that was so untidy that I just couldn't work in it. As I was there for a few days I tidied up a bit, remembering where everything had been so that I could untidy it when I left!

Although the children always tidy up you still need to finish the job to your own satisfaction. So, I had to see the children off the premises, then make sure that everything was tidy. Hmm, this was going to be tight, time-wise.

I must admit that it was twenty to four when I hurtled up the stairs to the cookery area, rather flustered and out of breath, to find all six children sitting quietly, awaiting my arrival. The looks on their faces said it all - well, they were all here on time, so where was I? One boy said nothing but just pointedly looked at his watch!

I apologised profusely but it wasn't exactly the best start, and I knew that this first session had to go well if there was any chance of the children coming back again.

I wanted the children to experience the food by smelling and tasting the finished article, but also by tasting the ingredients, where appropriate, along the way. I wanted them to do most of the work, after I had demonstrated a technique, even though this would mean slight accidents and mess.

I wanted them to learn about Health and Safety in the kitchen (common sense stuff really), and I wanted them to learn about nutrition and the dangers of junk food. Tips for shopping would come into it as well and, although I couldn't take them shopping, I pointed out the freshness of food and the bargains to look out for.

We would also compare prices of the ingredients we used. I particularly got them to work out the cost of making a meal from fresh, wholesome ingredients as compared with a ready meal that was full of unwanted additives. Most of all I wanted them to enjoy themselves.

The first thing they had to do to make Chocolate Crunch was to bash the Digestive biscuits into crumbs. (I never used a food processor as most of these children wouldn't have one at home.) They absolutely loved this and set about enthusiastically reducing the biscuits to the smallest crumbs I had ever seen. Melting the sugar, margarine and cocoa powder was relatively easy, but getting the right amount of Golden Syrup into the pan was another matter! Ah well, fingers were made for licking but I insisted that they had to wash their hands again!

The children were polite and very keen and the session went really well. I always got a few moans when it came to the washing up, but the threat of not being able to eat what we had made usually worked! Activities like cooking give lots of opportunities for talking and we discussed everything from current affairs to the meaning of life - well, maybe not quite that - but I think the children recognised that they could discuss things with me and that I would always be honest with them.

Of course the day came when the dreaded OFSTED descended on the school. I don't have much good to say about them, but it is an interesting fact that in thirty four years of teaching I was never inspected by them. The last school I worked at had an inspection two months before I started there and then one two months after I left! How lucky can you get!

Although I wasn't worried about anybody inspecting me because I was, in this instance, a volunteer doing an after-school club, I thought that they might show an interest. As I didn't want to let Mr Fox, the teachers and children down, I had prepared my own mini-curriculum with targets, methods, evaluations and all that stuff. (That isn't the word that first came to mind and I'm sure that you can think of a better one!)

At that time I did have a boy who had behavioural difficulties, but he wasn't too bad and hadn't given me any problems before.

When we cooked Spaghetti Bolognese we always ate it together, after setting the table properly, and with fruit juice to drink. (I ignored the comments of,

"Couldn't we have wine, Miss Young?"). We would prepare it all then I would say, "This really needs slow cooking in an oven for an hour in order to get a really rich delicious sauce."

As this would be at the end of the lesson the children would look so disappointed, particularly as I had said that we would eat a meal altogether. I soon took pity on them and pointed out that the oven had been on all during the lesson with, in best Blue Peter fashion, one I had prepared earlier at home.

Actually I only had to do that the first week because after that the second group ate the first meal, the third group ate the second one and so on.

For the meal I took in a tablecloth, serviettes, a small candelabra complete with candles, fruit squashes instead of wine, and some nice plates. The children always appreciated these little touches as it made them feel special and grown-up.

I had to show many of them how to set a table, and we did fancy things with the serviettes to make the table look posh.

I wanted to impress any OFSTED inspector who might stumble across us so I decided that particular week we would cook and eat the Spaghetti Bolognaise. Yes, I know, I was being a creep again!

The day came and I was so organised that it wasn't true. I was also a bit nervous as well, to tell the truth. The children were told to come as soon as they could at home time so we could get started and have plenty of time.

The meal had been cooked, the table set, and we had just started to eat. I was feeling quite relaxed now, as surely nobody would come to see us when the lesson was nearly over?

At that moment a woman whom I recognised as the Lay Inspector strolled past our table. She smiled at us, I held my breath, and then she carried on walking. Great, I was thinking, I've got away with it! Then I heard the boy with the behaviour problems, who had been as good as gold all lesson, pipe up with, "Do you think that lady would like some Spaghetti?"

I froze.

"It's a nice idea," I said quickly, "but I think that she's probably too busy."

"Well, shall I go and ask her, just in case she has got time?"

Never before had he shown such concern for another so who was I to nip this show of good manners in the bud?

"Yes, go on then," I managed to splutter, feeling fairly confident that she would refuse, and hoping that he wouldn't catch up with her anyway.

Not a bit of it! She came back and sat down with the children, while I hurriedly tried to find a plate of uncongealed Spaghetti and some meat sauce that the children had overlooked.

At least she started to talk to the children and soon we were all chatting away, and I started to feel that I could relax.

They say never work with children or animals as you never know what they are going to do next. They are so right!

The Inspector asked the children if they had enjoyed their day.

The boy who was responsible for this situation suddenly blurted out, "No, I've had a crummy day!"

Well, at least he had toned his language down, but my sixth sense, which all teachers have, alerted me to the possible danger if we pursued this any further. "Would anybody like some more juice?" I heard myself say in a slightly hysterical voice.

Nobody answered. This other conversation would be much more interesting.

"Yeah, I had a really lousy time in PE," he went on. "You know that Wesley who's a right nutter?"

The other children all nodded in agreement.

"Would anybody like some more sauce?" I came out with, in an even higher and more hysterical voice, while looking at the empty casserole dish.

Nobody answered me, and I resigned myself to the inevitable.

"Well, he kicked me when I hadn't done nuthin' to him, then he punched Michael, so I went and nutted him!"

There was a stunned silence while I refrained from asking whether there had been an OFSTED Inspector in the lesson. I also wondered whether this Inspector would think it worth her while following this up.

"Yeah, and then you'll never guess what!"

But I had had enough and I firmly got to my feet and said, "Goodness, look at the clock! Doesn't time fly when you're enjoying yourself! Your parents will be up here soon wondering where you are!" (I always witter on when I'm nervous!)

Fortunately the Inspector took the hint and, after thanking us for an interesting time(!), headed off leaving a crumpled nervous wreck behind.

She didn't follow this conversation up, which was a great relief to me.

That reminds me of a time when I was teaching five and six year olds in a mainstream class. After we had done the register in the morning, the children were encouraged to tell us some news about their family, or something interesting that they had done.

One little girl put her hand up and said, "My Mummy and Daddy were laughing last night."

"Oh yes?" I said innocently, not realising the implications of this seemingly innocuous statement.

The other children looked rather bored.

"Yes, they were upstairs and Daddy was tickling Mummy, that's why she was laughing."

Oh, oh, my sixth sense kicked in just in time. The other children started to look rather more interested.

"Well, that's lovely, now does anybody else have any news?"

The children's hands all stayed resolutely down.

"Then Daddy threw Mummy's nightie down the stairs and …"

I had heard enough and went into witter mode.

"Now, let's see what we are going to do today shall we?"

The children all looked very disappointed and I could see that she was going to be very popular at break time, as she regaled the rest of the class with what had happened next. And they were all so young as well! The funny thing is that I occasionally see the couple involved, and every time I do, I can't help but think of that day!

Anyway, to get back to the Cookery Club; as I headed out of school that evening, laden down, and much later than usual, having done all the clearing up, I bumped into Mr Fox.

You always hope people notice when you go that extra mile and although you don't expect thanks every week, it was really good when he looked me in the eye and said, "I just want you to know, Pam, that we are very grateful to you for running this Cookery Club. It's another activity which we can offer the children and help them to learn some life skills. They really enjoy it, you know, so thank you."

That was all I needed.

§

I felt that we must do something to reward the supermarket for providing all the ingredients every week, and to say thank you to the very pleasant staff.

When we baked buns and cakes I suggested to the children that we make a cake for the supermarket staff. They could decorate it as they wished and then I would take it to them on my way to work the next day.

I believe that children are generous beings who love to do things for other people, so, as long as they could take home some buns, I was pretty sure that they would agree.

I had lots of cake decorations in my basket at my next shopping trip.

"It looks like the children are going to have fun making a cake!" The assistant grinned at me.

"Yes," I replied. "Let's hope it's edible!"

The children had great fun decorating their own buns, but really went to town on the cake. It wasn't the most fantastic sponge I had ever seen but it was edible. I think it was their enthusiasm which was the problem because they just didn't know how to mix the ingredients gently.

They went at it like whirling dervishes, and folding the flour in was a nightmare. Still, they had done their best, and they were really enjoying themselves.

The ideas for the decoration looked as if they had come from a horror movie - there was a lot of red around, and the original white icing had disappeared beneath a blanket of every kind of sweet and topping you could think of. I had to restrain the children from putting on a second layer!

Eventually they pronounced that they were satisfied, and they stood proudly as I lowered it very carefully into a tin, promising to take good care of it.

The next day I carried it very carefully into the supermarket and went over to the Customer Services desk. Fortunately, it was the same lady as I had seen before. She had a rather quizzical look on her face as I approached, carrying a large tin.

Wait until you see what I've got in here, I thought, trying not to break out into hysterical laughter.

I took the lid off and watched her face. The smile vanished for a second, but she soon recovered and managed to regain her composure.

"The children wanted to say thank you for providing us with all the ingredients for our Cookery Club, so they have baked you a cake."

Then I hastily added, "They did all the decoration themselves."

I didn't want her to think I had anything to do with it!

She was obviously struggling with her emotions as although she opened her mouth, nothing came out.

I moved closer to her and said, in a very quiet voice, "Please feel free to do exactly what you want with it - if you want to dispose of it I shall quite understand." Well, the children would never have known, would they?

However, she drew herself up and retorted, "I wouldn't dream of doing that. I'm sure we will really enjoy it. Please say a big thank you to the children." Right, that was me told then!

As I walked down the corridor at school the children from the Cookery Club swarmed round me.

"Did they like the cake?" they demanded.

"They loved it," I replied truthfully. "They couldn't wait to try some, and they thought that the icing and decorations were particularly striking."

Their heads went up and they went confidently down the corridor, knowing that they were Cooks, real Cooks!

Every group baked a cake for the staff at the supermarket and I took every one of them in. Each person I presented the cake to was grateful and enthusiastic, as though I had just presented them with the crown jewels! I don't suppose they ever realised how they made a difference to those children's lives, so I hereby put it on record, with my thanks to the staff at that supermarket in York.

The only time that I had a problem with a child in the Cookery Club was with a boy called Nick. He was known to be a difficult child and the Staff did their best to persuade me not to accept him. But I was pleased he had said that he wanted to come and I wanted to give him a chance.

The children knew that their behaviour in a kitchen

had to be spot on and that if they misbehaved they would be out. I always meant what I said in any situation with a child and I always carried out any stipulations that I made.

If I said to a child, "If you do A, then B will happen," then B would happen, and most came to recognise that, and would abide by it.

During Nick's first session I could feel that he was 'bubbling', but he managed to hold it together.

However, during the second session he just 'lost it' and started fooling around with the knife, which wasn't really sharp but was sharp enough.

The other children looked at me, expecting me to do something, as they knew the rules and the reasons for them.

"Put the knife down, please, Nick," I said calmly.

He smirked at me and stood defiantly with the knife still in his hand.

"I won't ask you again, Nick, but if you don't put it down you won't be allowed to come to our club again."

I nearly threatened him with the Headteacher, but I wanted to sort this out myself, hopefully resolving it so that he could stay with us, and that we wouldn't become enemies, in his mind, not mine.

One of the main tenets of good behaviour management is to avoid confrontations at all costs. I think that I had become fairly skilled at that, primarily by using humour, or by pretending that their course of action was the one you were going to take anyway. That didn't involve a climb down by me as the child didn't know what I was going to do.

Sometimes, if things had gone badly with a child, or

I was feeling tired or unhappy about something, then a confrontation could become inevitable, but this was rare, thank goodness. It always ended badly as the child had no way out of the situation, so would blow his top, and any work in that session would be out of the question, while I would be racked by guilt and would probably end up with a headache and a feeling of failure.

Nick knew that I meant business so, with a scowl, he put down the knife, but turned away from us all and stood simmering in the corner of the room.

I hadn't got the time to talk to him, but thought that it was much better to leave him be, so that he could come round in his own time.

As we carried on there was a shout, "I'm not staying here! I'm off!"

Oh, heck! Now where was he going? The door was flung open and he flounced out, almost straight into the arms of Bob, one of the Year Six teachers! Bob looked at me enquiringly.

"Nick's just going to the toilet, aren't you?" I said firmly, looking him in the eye. Well, he could well have been. Children with behaviour problems often spent a lot of time in the toilets!

And I really didn't want him to get into trouble again. Nick mumbled something then shot off towards the cloakrooms. Thank goodness, he reappeared a few minutes later and he carried on as if nothing had happened. I'm sure that Bob would have been around just to see that things were OK, but I never had any trouble with Nick again, and he actually completed the course, against all the odds.

I ran the Cookery Club for a year, but after that I gave

it up, albeit reluctantly. It was very demanding, and by the time I had made sure that the kitchen we used was spotless and tidy it was late, and so I was always late home.

It wasn't just the time involved at school either. I spent quite a while getting the shopping in, making sure that the relevant paperwork had been completed, chasing children up who came a couple of times and then dropped out. Some of them didn't know the meaning of the word 'commitment', I'm afraid.

I feel that I was a bit of a trailblazer, though, as now celebrity Chefs and other Cooks go into school and do just what I did.

I have just heard on the radio today that the government thinks it would be a good idea for children to have compulsory Cookery classes, in order to combat the rise in obesity levels. But who was it who squeezed Cookery lessons out of the curriculum? We all said that it was a very short-sighted thing to do, but I'm afraid that each government always thinks that it knows better than the teachers. Well, it doesn't! I can still remember many of the things that I was taught in my Domestic Science lessons at school. (I'll never forget the teacher telling me to drink the raw egg that I had left over from a lesson, and standing over me to make sure that I did! It was the only time in my school life that I defied a teacher, and I still think that I was right to do so!)

"Never leave your dishcloth in a bundle as the germs will flourish in the damp, warm environment; always hang it up."

"Always feel proud enough of a piece of work to put your name on it."

(The teacher at this point went and got a kettle out of the stock cupboard and showed us the name of the manufacturer - Swan.)

"If you aren't proud enough to put your name on what you've done, start again!"

If I could remember all these things thirty five years later, then hopefully some of what I was saying might stick in these children's minds. One of the scary things about teaching is that many children hang on your every word and, not only do you have to be careful about what you say, but what you say can influence a child in their future life, hopefully in a positive way.

Sometimes, on Parents' Evening a parent would say how their child had come home and repeated what I had said. One Mum once said, laughing, that they got fed up with hearing, "Mrs Young says that..." Apparently my word was law, according to their offspring!

§

So, I gave up the Cookery classes, but I still continued to cook with individual children or small groups throughout my career.

From four year olds to eleven year olds, I never knew a child who didn't like to cook, and I think it a shame now that many parents are too busy or too exhausted to teach their children to cook, if, indeed, they themselves can produce a good home-cooked meal from scratch. And no, I'm not talking about heating something up in a microwave!

I always thought it was very important to teach the

children life skills, whether it be cooking, filling in forms or wiring a plug. For many children, mainly those with learning difficulties, the delights of the Amazonian Rainforest, or how to write in different genres are just not relevant to them. No wonder they get bored and switch off, or worst still, develop behaviour problems.

Oh, in case you're wondering, here is the recipe for Chocolate Crunch:

Ingredients
425g Digestive biscuits
2 tablespoons Golden Syrup
2 tablespoons caster sugar
3 tablespoons cocoa
210g margarine
200g milk/plain chocolate, as preferred
You will also need a 9 inch square cake tin, greased.

Method
1. Wash your hands.
2. Put on your apron.
3. Crumble the biscuits and put into a big bowl.
4. Melt the rest of the ingredients, **except the chocolate,** in a pan, but do not let this boil.
5. Pour this mixture over the biscuit crumbs and mix together well.
6. Flatten the mixture into the tin and leave to set.
7. Break the chocolate into a heatproof basin and put it over a pan of boiling water, taken off the heat. When melted, pour over the mixture and leave to set.
8. Cut into 16 pieces.

13

"You'll Be Alright, Mrs Young!"

Not all the children I taught had behaviour problems. I taught some really lovely girls, although they were in the minority.

One of them was called Natalie and I started working with her when she was in Year Six ie ten years old. This was another classic case of the help being put in later rather than sooner, but at least she did get the help. She didn't have any major problems, but had just got a bit behind with her Literacy skills.

From Day One we hit it off, and after some of the other children I was asked to teach, my lessons with Natalie were so easy and relaxed. She had a good sense of humour too, so that helped a lot. She tried hard, was never awkward or stubborn, and made a lot of progress with her reading and spelling. The latter was her biggest problem, but she never gave up and always took on board everything I taught her. If only I could have had more pupils like her! I looked forward to our sessions, as I think she did.

The day came when all the Tutors had to be observed teaching, something that Classroom Teachers had put up with for a while. Obviously it is not something that you look forward to, but all our bosses made it as bearable as possible. We were allowed to choose the lesson to be observed in, and the person who was coming to watch me was Angela, who I liked very much. She was lovely to work with, was very down to earth, and had a good sense of humour.

I was very nervous when my turn came. I had chosen Natalie to teach, and my planning was very thorough. Wasn't it always, I hear you say?

I had told Natalie that someone would be observing us, but I had emphasised it was me they were coming to assess. Children have become so used to being assessed and tested that she had assumed she was the target for this observation.

I collected Natalie from the hall where she was having a drama lesson, and I obviously looked rather scared because she put her hand on my arm and said reassuringly, "You'll be alright, Mrs Young, don't be nervous."

I smiled weakly but she was right, thank goodness, and the lesson went very well. It couldn't have gone any other way with Natalie and Angela in my corner. I got a good report and Natalie and I celebrated with a glass of fruit juice and a chocolate biscuit afterwards!

I later found out that Angela had been very nervous as well, although I don't know why!

Natalie made excellent progress, not surprisingly, and towards the end of her time at the school the Educational Psychologist came to assess her. Every child who had a statement always had to have an Annual Review meeting, their progress had to be assessed, and new targets and planning had to be laid down.

Her assessment showed that she had made excellent progress, although I couldn't claim much of the glory. Natalie fully deserved the praise, as she had made excellent use of my time and efforts, and with supportive parents we couldn't go wrong.

She was very good at dancing and I took great delight in following her excellent progress in her musical activities.

Judy was also a delightful girl but she did have significant learning problems. It took ages for her to get a Statement and, like Natalie, it was better late than never. She was always smiling, laughing and joking, and was very aware of other people's feelings. She had impeccable manners and was always anxious to help adults and other children alike. She, too, had a supportive mother, who tried hard to help her daughter. She also had a rare capacity in children with Special Needs - she could laugh at herself and frequently did.

That was in stark contrast to most of the children who were extremely prickly and would have a major paddy if they got one tiny, little thing wrong. I remember one particular boy who was like this. Assessing him was a nightmare because as soon as he got the first word wrong in the spellings, you could see him stiffen and his whole body would droop with dismay.

He would then, after the next mistake, become very surly, until, in the end he would refuse to go on. Oh, how I dreaded assessing him, and yet I had to do it to find out which words he could spell and which he couldn't. All the agony was worth it in the end, as he also made excellent progress. By the time he left the school he had almost caught up with his peers, and five years later he got six good GCSE passes.

A year after Natalie and Judy went to Comprehensive School, their SBAT Tutor there, a lovely lady named Sandy, invited me to go to their school for afternoon tea to meet up with them again, and see how much progress they had made.

Instead of finding two lovely young girls, I found

two lovely young ladies, and it was a delight to see them again and to spend the afternoon with them.

I quite often liaised with the Comprehensive Schools and visited them for various reasons, although I usually found them to be intimidating places. All those huge young men towering above me - and I mean the pupils, not the Staff - and walking down a corridor at break time was terrifying.

In July, all Year Six pupils visited the Comprehensive School they were to start at that September. The Staff put on various exciting activities for them, they had their lunch there, met the Staff, and became more familiar with the layout of the place. All these schools were so big to me that I needed a map or a minder so that I didn't get hopelessly lost.

Nearly all of my pupils were very nervous about this day, as they didn't have the confidence which other pupils had. I could understand this myself as I feel very much like that about new things.

So, I devised a plan where I would take my SEN children on a day in June, just before the official Induction Day, and we would meet the SENCo and other Support Staff, and see any specially designated SEN rooms where they could go for help.

Usually, at my suggestion, the SENCo would find a pupil who would take them on a tour of the school and answer any questions they had. If a teacher did this, the children would just clam up and never say a word, so we thought that they might talk to somebody just a bit older than themselves, and who they might even know.

Meanwhile, the SENCo and I could have a very frank talk about their new charges, and I could pass on vital information. The SENCos appreciated this visit as much as the children did, and it became an acknowledged part of a good transition plan for SEN children.

I once rang up the newly appointed SENCo of a school which had amalgamated with another school. I had never had to deal with a male SENCo before and when I asked him if I could bring three children with SEN on a visit, he was rather offhand.

"They'll be coming in July with all the other pupils, won't they?" he enquired.

I explained to him what the benefits would be of them coming before that day.

"I suppose it's alright," he said grudgingly. I knew why he was being so reluctant. As a new SENCo he must have wondered what had hit him.

Anyway, I wouldn't give up and we fixed a date in June. To his credit he rang me afterwards and said that he now appreciated why I wanted the visit, and that he had found it most useful.

Next year when I rang he was very enthusiastic!

The most significant visit to a Comprehensive School by me came as a result of a question posed to a child at the end of her Annual Review meeting by an Educational Psychologist, Tony, whose friendly manner and astute observations I admired.

Heidi had been another of those lovely co-operative girls who posed no problems, and I had enjoyed teaching her.

She had left her Primary School some years ago and had made excellent progress at her Comprehensive School.

So, at this Review meeting Tony said to her, "Who,

of all the people who have taught you, would you like to come and see how well you have done?"

Heidi thought for a moment and then said, "Mrs Young."

I can get quite tearful recalling this even now!

So Tony came beetling over to our school and asked me whether I would like to go and see her. Would I like to? Just try stopping me!

The only time that was suitable for everybody was Friday afternoon, possibly the most scary time to pick in a Comprehensive School! The lesson was one on needlework, possibly an even more scary lesson to pick, with all those needles!

Heidi showed me her work and I marvelled at the lovely young lady who had produced such fantastic things, and who spoke confidently to me, although she was a bit shy to start with.

She was interested in what I had been doing in the intervening years too, and soon we were chatting away together as two adults. Some of her friends came to talk to me as well, and I was impressed with their friendliness and maturity. The lesson was better than I had hoped, and the standard of their work was much higher than anything that we had done at school in our needlework classes.

Heidi also did well in her GCSEs and I am hopeful she will have a reasonable job by now.

14

"Can We Buy George A Computer?"

We all know that most children love to go to parties, but from my experience, most children love to **give** parties too, and are not always as self-centred as some people would have you believe.

George was a Year Six pupil and the only Year Six child I had at that time. He worked with Kerry-Anne, but she was in Year Five, and so he was the only pupil to be leaving our school and going on to the local Comprehensive School.

All the other children I taught at that school knew George and he was a quiet, but popular boy. I always bought the Year Six pupils a little present when they left and, knowing that money was in short supply in his house, I had bought George a school set with pencils, erasers, Maths equipment etc.

I wondered one day about having a farewell party for him, and if I took this set apart the other children could wrap up one item each and present it to him. They could write a little message on a label as well, but then I quickly realised that I was getting carried away - SEN children voluntarily writing?

As I had each group that day I asked them all how they would feel about giving George a surprise party. They all said that it was a brilliant idea, in fact the best thing since sliced bread! Now, getting them to keep it a secret would be a major achievement, but I thought it was worth a try.

As an Infants Teacher I had become quite used to being told by an excited Infant at Christmas time, "My mum says that we're going to get you a present for Christmas but it's a surprise so I mustn't tell you!"

They would then be on the verge of telling me what the present was, so I had to be very tactful and change the subject!

Every child I asked that day was thrilled by the prospect of giving George a party. I pointed out that they would have to work hard to get everything ready for him, as I wasn't going to do it all myself. That was the deal - no contribution from them, no party.

The children were brilliant. They fired questions at me, covering all the relevant details and more.

"Could we write the invitations?" Now that was a surprise - did I hear the 'w' word?

"Can we make the invitations?"

"Can we make him a cake?"

"Can we have balloons?"

"Can we get him some presents and wrap them up?"

"Can we write on the label?"

Now I must have been dreaming - that was the second time that I'd heard the 'w' word!

"Can we play games and have prizes?"

Then the questions became a little more unrealistic.

"Can we invite the whole school?"

"Can I bring my dog, 'cos she loves parties?"

"Could we buy George a computer? I know it's big but I don't mind wrapping it!"

"Can we all have hot dogs and pizzas and chicken nuggets and fish and chips, that's my very, very favourite thing?"

"Oh, and jelly and ice cream and a huge cake and buns and biscuits and…"

This was getting out of hand so I tried to rein them in a little without curbing their enthusiasm. We came up with some realistic plans and I promised that the next day we would start wrapping presents and writing gift tags.

Asking every teacher for permission to 'borrow' the children at a different time from usual for the party was time-consuming, and finding a day that would be suitable for everyone wasn't easy, but eventually a date was fixed, and the children and teachers were all sworn to secrecy. I had thought that George would probably hear about it five minutes after we had all agreed the plans, but I was proved wrong. I should have had more faith.

As I have said before, finding a room to teach in was always a problem, and this was in the days before that particular Headteacher had made me my own room. So, I staggered into school the next day, laden down with presents, wrapping paper, scissors, gift tags, Sellotape and card, ready for work, and in dire need of a room with a big table and lots of space. Hmm! I was usually just grateful for a door and four walls.

At last I stumbled into the music room. Yes, there was lots of space, a big table and there was nobody else in it. I looked on the room's timetable and joy, oh, joy, there was nobody timetabled for that lesson. I moved all my stuff in, went to collect my first two groups (I thought it would be quicker if we merged groups), and soon the scissors ("Just be careful what you're doing with those."), the wrapping paper ("Er, I don't think you need two sheets to wrap up a pencil sharpener!") and Sellotape ("No, I'd rather you put that on the present than on your mouth, and certainly not on Kayleigh's mouth!") were all being gainfully employed to make George's last day a very special and memorable one.

The table was hidden under a mountain of paper when I suddenly heard just what I hadn't wanted to hear - the sound of a class of children heading towards the room. I glanced at the timetable and saw the reassuring blank space for this time.

The door opened and Mary, a teacher with whom I got on very well, came to an abrupt halt while thirty-two children cannoned into each other, as they all realised that there was a problem.

"Ah, Mrs Young, sorry, I didn't realise that you were in here."

She looked very contrite and I could see what was coming.

"You see, I have to practise for our Assembly and there's somebody in the hall and I need the space and…"

She smiled sweetly at me.

"I'll owe you one!"

I turned and looked in despair at the 'mess' on the table, and at the children's anxious faces.

Just then Luke's eager voice piped up, "Don't worry, Miss Young, we'll pick up the table and carry it into the corridor."

The other children nodded in agreement and relieved smiles broke out all round.

"I'm not sure that the table will go through the doorway, Luke, but it was a good idea and …"

Without waiting to hear what my next objection was going to be, the six children picked up the table, squeezed it through the doorway with much shouted encouragement from the waiting children, and I found that my lesson had transferred very smoothly out into the corridor.

The children, bless 'em, just carried on and soon, with the presents wrapped, were voluntarily writing good luck messages to George. This, from children who, faced with having to write in an ordinary lesson would protest loudly and do anything to avoid it. I've always believed that if a child sees a purpose in something they will generally get on and do it.

I once read a story of a teacher who had gone into the pub in a village where he used to teach. There, playing darts, was one of his former pupils who had been hopeless at Maths. He challenged him to a game of darts, and the teacher was astonished to find that subtracting numbers from his score was a piece of cake for the young man. He gently reminded him that Maths had never been his strong point.

"Ah, but I need to subtract now to play darts," came the answer. "I never needed all that Algebra stuff, did I?"

He had a point.

By the end of the session we had six parcels in various degrees of tidiness, each with a very nice little note attached along the lines of;

"Gud look, Gorge."

"I hop thet yew wil be hapy at yor nuw scule."

"I wil mis you."

"I like yuw, Jorj."

"Hav a gud tiem."

"Im sori thet yor leeving."

I didn't change a single one.

The children were very excited about the coming party and I was nattered every day.

"Is it today?"

That would be the first question, followed by, "Well, how about tomorrow then?"

The day of the party arrived at last.

Most of the children had volunteered their mums to make cakes and provide crisps etc, but fortunately I decided to supply most of the food myself. It was just as well really, as only one child actually brought something.

"Oh, I forgot!"

"My Mum didn't have any money!"

"My Mum said she didn't have time!"

The excuses rolled in and I was sorry for the children who were obviously disappointed about their lack of food, but they were reassured when they saw what I had got with me.

As for the party games, I must admit that I was being a bit self-indulgent, and we were going to play games that I had enjoyed when I was their age. Who could ever forget the joys of 'Flap the Kipper' where you had to flap a piece of card up and down to create a draught which would move the tissue paper 'kipper'? There was quite a knack involved but no physical strength, so even the smallest child could win. Of course the potential for silences and withdrawals into the corners of the room to sulk because, in their eyes, they had failed, were enormous, and my skills as a Special Needs Teacher would be really stretched by the end of the party, but I was prepared for that. A couple of headache tablets and a lie-down in a dark-ened room should do the trick!

Pass the Parcel should be alright, as I had wrapped a sweet in between every third layer, with a bigger prize in the middle. A bit of judicious observation and swift stopping of the music - no, not cheating - should ensure that each child would win something.

You could see why my planning had to be thoughtful and meticulous, otherwise World War Three might break out, or seven children might end up thoroughly depressed, with not a jot of self-esteem between them. Games like Musical Statues and Musical Bumps would be OK, as long as I curtailed things and had three winners, then immediately restarted the game.

I collected the children at break time and, unusually for them, they quite happily gave up part of the only time when they didn't feel under pressure. They were so excited and their only aim was to give George a really good send off.

We all hid behind a wall in the cloakroom while I bribed a mate of George's to go and tell him that I wanted to see him. It's amazing how the sight and smell of a bun will persuade a loud-mouthed, unco-operative eleven year old boy to co-operate. I felt pretty sure that George would come willingly as he would have found out about the party but no, I couldn't have been more wrong.

I could see that he was coming very reluctantly, as he had been playing football, and the look of surprise on his face as we all leapt out at him was a dead give-away.

"Surprise! Surprise!"

"Party time!"

"Thingy - it's a party for you!" (Well, some of us had poor memories!)

The look of shock on George's face, and then the bemused grin which appeared as the children grabbed his arms and dragged him off to the room where the party was to be held, was proof that he hadn't known about it. And if a member of Staff wanted to bring their class to that room, I wasn't moving!

Mind you, I had checked with every single teacher but we all knew that a visit from the School Nurse/Speech Therapist could throw things into disarray, but this time I was not giving way!

I couldn't help saying to him as we approached the room, "Did you really not know about the party or are you just being a superb actor?"

George grinned. "Honest, Miss Young, I got the shock of me life when you all jumped out! I nearly 'ad 'eart failure!"

The first thing that the children wanted to do was to give George their presents. Each one solemnly took him their gift and read out what they had written on the tag. I must say that I had tears in my eyes and George looked visibly moved. He seemed to be pleased with every single item and he thanked each child in turn.

This, for me, is all part of the 'hidden curriculum' and is just as important as the National Curriculum. Things like doing something for another person, saying please and thank you, being aware of another's feelings, helping a child who has fallen over in the playground. The list is endless.

"When are we having the food?" Six voices, almost in unison directed George towards the food table.

"Why don't we play one game first?" I said firmly.

The children acquiesced but I knew that one game was all I dared do. I chose to start with 'Flap the Kipper'. The children lined up with their respective bits of cardboard, with the tissue paper 'kippers' in front of them. I had to start them really quickly before there was a false start, and soon they were flapping for all they were worth. It was interesting, though, because the older and bigger boys obviously thought that brute strength was needed, whereas Lucy and Courtney, two smaller and younger girls, soon realised that their lack of height actually helped them, as the 'kippers' moved more quickly with the air going underneath them, rather than coming from above.

The boys looked on incredulously as Lucy and her 'kipper' reached the end of the room first.

"Oh, Miss Young, that's not fair, she's…"

Before he had time to say anything else, I quickly whipped the cover off the table and announced, "Come and get some food!"

I was nearly knocked over in the rush, but the boys forgot their grievances as they had a competition to see how much food they could pile onto a small paper plate. Really, the Guinness Book of Records would have been interested!

When the plates had nothing but crumbs on them, I managed to interest them in another game, this time Musical Bumps. But there was too much scope for querying my decisions in that game, so we quickly moved on to Pass the Parcel. That was much better, particularly as they all won something, due, I freely admit, to me fiddling it!

By this time I was becoming exhausted, and I'd had enough. I only persuaded them to go when I pointed out it was lunch time and time to eat again.

The party was a huge success though, and all the

children had a great time, although I would doubt whether any of them actually ate any lunch.

As the others went happily off to the dining hall or playground and their envious friends, George hung back.

"That were ace, Miss Young," he said quietly. "Thanks."

George was a boy of few words but he had said all the right ones there.

"It's a pleasure, George," I replied. "We all enjoyed ourselves so much preparing it for you because we all think so much about you. I shall miss you."

He smiled at me again, picked up all his presents and went out of the room. Right at that moment I felt a real sense of loss.

That reminds me of the Summer when all my pupils at that school, bar one, left to go on to Secondary School. They were all great children as well and I was dreading saying goodbye to them.

At the end of term Assembly I managed to keep myself in check and held the tears back. As soon as we came out I went back to my room, shut the door and started to cry. After a minute or so there came a knock at the door and without waiting for an answer the door opened, and the Secretary stood there with Luke, one of my pupils, at her side. He was holding a camera.

"Luke wondered if he could take your photo, Mrs Young."

They both looked at my tear-stained face then, "Perhaps we'll come back this afternoon," she said hastily and backed out of the room, dragging a wide-eyed Luke with her.

"Can We Buy George A Computer?"

George's party was only the first of many Year Six leaving parties, and each child knew that they would be given a party too. After all, they had earned it by helping to organise everyone else's.

When a friend of mine, Jack, a retired teacher, heard me talking about the parties, he offered to come and entertain all the children with some magic tricks, followed by a juggling workshop. At first I wondered how these children with low self-esteem would cope with trying a new skill, but I needn't have worried. Jack was very patient and was well aware of their needs.

It also helped that, despite taking part in four workshops, I was always the worst there! I never made any progress and the children delighted in trying to help me. And no, I wasn't pretending to be useless. It just came naturally!

The first time Jack came he insisted on involving me in almost every trick, especially those in which I ended up looking a fool or getting wet.

When he produced an egg and asked me to catch it, Sam, who of course had had an egg thrown at him by me, was beside himself with excitement! Normally a quiet, reticent child, he jumped up and down with excitement, shouting, "It's alright Miss Young, don't worry, I think it will be 'ard-boiled!"

The others looked disappointed, as the thought of their teacher being covered in raw egg would have been the highlight of the day.

Nevertheless, I managed to catch it three times before I dropped it so that the suspense was kept up for a little longer. Jack was a huge success and the workshop went extremely well. Children who would normally not volunteer for a thing were leaping up and down in their urge to be picked by Jack to help him with a trick or some juggling.

When we worked with a partner I chose Heidi who was the youngest there and would maybe need a bit of extra nurturing. After a few minutes she had sussed me out. She decided to teach me.

"Miss Young, hold your hands higher!"

"Miss Young, not like that!"

"Oh, well done, Miss Young!"

"Look, everyone, Miss Young caught it then!"

For once in her life she was the top dog and she revelled in it. She was so patient with me, too, and never got exasperated.

Nobody mentioned food until I drew their attention to it. I could see that Jack was flagging a bit and I certainly was. As soon as they had done their plague of locusts act the children started to advance on Jack with cries of, "Can we have another go, please?"

"Do that thing with the egg again, go on, please!"

"Show us that trick with the balls again, please!"

"Can I throw an egg at Miss Young, please?"

I always insisted that the children should say please and thank you at all times, even when they were beside themselves with excitement. If they forgot, a hard stare and raised eyebrows quickly made them remember.

Eventually, I persuaded the children that it was lunch time, and the thought of eating again made them realise that the party was over.

Not one of the children forgot to say thank you to Jack, and to me.

As we sat down with a cup of coffee, Jack said to me,

"I thought these children were supposed to have Special Needs, be lacking in self-confidence and be really shy!"

"Yes, well, usually they are," I protested. "It's not every day that they have such an inspiring teacher!"

Jack gave me an old-fashioned look and I knew what he meant. I was the 'bread and butter' teacher while he was the icing on the cake. He came back every Summer for the leavers' party until I left that school, and I shall always be grateful to him for giving the children such a great time. As I had to point out to him, though, I was his only failure!

15

She's My Best Friend – And I Hate Her!

The school bell rang at noon. Oh great, I thought, lunch time!

"Right," I said to Jessica. "Time to eat. Or do you have to go out to play first and then go for your lunch?"

She lifted her head and looked me in the eye. "I have to go out to play first - it's not lunch time for me."

"Well, that's good, isn't it? You can go out and see your friends and have a run around."

I knew that I was on a very sticky wicket from the miserable look on her face.

"Oh yeah, it's freezing cold out there and my best friend isn't talking to me anymore and I'd rather stay in here with you."

Goodness, I thought, things must be bad.

"Well, what about the dinner ladies? They'll talk to you and find somebody for you to play with."

"Yeah, and if I start walking round with them, everybody will know that I haven't got any friends and they'll make fun of me."

I opened my mouth to say something, but before I could speak, Jessica went on, "And don't say 'sticks and stones may break my bones but names will never hurt me' because that just isn't true, Mrs Young. It hurts much more when somebody calls you names."

I tried to look as if that thought had been the last thing on my mind, but had the feeling that I was failing miserably.

By this time she was nearly in tears and I was at a loss to know what to do with her. I had to be at another school by one o'clock, eat my sandwiches and prepare for my lessons.

"Look Jessica, I'll have a think and see what I can do, but I'm afraid I have to go now. I'll have a word with your teacher and tell her that you're feeling a bit unhappy."

"Yeah," she sighed and slowly got out of her chair. "Yeah, right."

She dragged herself out of the room and I started to put my things away. The thing was that Jessica was a lovely, cheerful girl usually, and I had thought that she had lots of friends.

Maybe she was having a difficult time at home or was just in a bad mood, but whatever it was I could not put her out of my mind.

I found her teacher and told her what Jessica had said. She promised to keep an eye on her and I rushed off to my next school.

Part of my job was to liaise with the Class Teachers about my pupils in their classes. Although this could be quite time consuming and not always easy to achieve, it was a very important aspect of my work, so had to be done.

Sometimes it was a question of reporting that a child wasn't feeling well, or that their behaviour had been very challenging (which is the politically correct way of saying they had been very naughty or annoying), or, more usually, that they had been very successful at something, and that progress was being made.

Then again, it could be the scenario that you dreaded; when a child disclosed something very serious that needed reporting as soon as possible to the SENCo or Headteacher. The most disturbing thing that a child would want to tell you was that they were being sexually abused, although they wouldn't use those exact words, of course. That never happened to me, but it did happen to a friend of mine, and it was a very traumatic time for all involved.

The worst time for me was when I was teaching a young boy aged nine years old. He happened to be on his own with me that day, as the boy who worked with him was absent. He was a lovely, co-operative child and he was an excellent role model for the other boy who had behaviour problems. I knew that something was wrong, as he seemed to be very moody and uneasy.

"Is there anything wrong?" I asked solicitously.

" No!" came the answer rather too quickly.

"OK," I said quietly, "but I hope that you know that you can tell me if there is something troubling you and I'll see if I can sort it out."

There was silence and I let the matter drop. After a while he looked at me and said the words that I would rather have not heard.

"If I tell you something, you won't tell anybody else, will you?"

I was always honest with the children.

"No, love, I can't promise that. I might have to tell Mr Smith (the Headteacher) if I think it is serious, and I think it **is** serious, isn't it?"

He nodded miserably. "Yes," he whispered.

I waited for him to speak again. He then told me about the violence he was experiencing at home and how unhappy he was. There is always the chance that you are dealing with a fertile imagination, but I didn't believe it was so in this case. I had never known him to be devious or to tell lies.

I told him I would have to find Mr Smith and tell him what I had heard, and that something would be done to try to help him. I reluctantly took him back to his classroom, and prayed fervently that the Head was in that day. Fortunately, he was and I unburdened myself to him.

He listened attentively and then promised that he would go and see the boy immediately. Meanwhile, I had to write a statement, detailing everything that the boy had said, sign it, and let him have it before I left the school. It would make me late for my next lesson in another school, but so be it.

In fact, in the end things were sorted out, and I heard very little else about it, much to my relief.

That night I couldn't get Jessica out of my mind, and the more I thought about it the more convinced I became that I could do something about it. Why should she have to go out in the cold and stand around on her own? How many other children were there who felt exactly the same?

I decided to approach the SENCo, a good friend, and see what she thought about me running a lunchtime club, where any of the children could come to my room and chat, play games, colour pictures in or just do what they wanted.

I could only manage to run it once a week, but that would be better than nothing.

Teresa, the SENCo, was very enthusiastic, and with the Headteacher's permission I set about organising it.

Jessica was the first child I told and I asked her to help me to set it up. She swelled with pride and perked up considerably, promising to spread the word amongst the other children.

The next Tuesday I sat in my room at lunch time, wondering if any children would come and join me. By a quarter past twelve, I was wondering how many more girls I could fit into my small room, and by half past twelve there was an overflow group out in the corridor!

By one o'clock I had managed to crawl into the staff room, where somebody had taken pity on me and made me a restoring cup of tea.

The girls (no boys, but that was to be expected) had chatted, laughed, coloured in pictures and played games. It was a bitterly cold day and I was well aware that many had come just to get out of the cold, but even so it was a great success. Little did I know what I had started that day. It became known as Mrs Young's Drop In Club (not Dropping Club as many insisted on calling it. Goodness knows what their parents thought we were doing!)

When it was Christmas, Easter, St Valentine's Day or some other special time, we made cards and did other Craft activities. Easter bonnets were a favourite, and by then we had one or two boys joining in. When they wanted to make a bonnet I always felt a bit worried and tried to convince myself, and them, that they were making them for their mums or sisters. One boy insisted that it was for him and what was more, he was going to wear it when he left my room. I had to take him on one side and convince him that this would not be a good idea, as he would be mercilessly teased and the other children would laugh at him. He took that on board but I was concerned for him and, naturally it was yet another thing to tell his teacher. I wonder what became of him, although I have a pretty good idea.

When I left that particular school and did more work at another school, I didn't carry on with a lunch time group at first. It was so demanding because I never got a proper break during the entire day, and the preparation and clearing up made it a very time-consuming and exhausting activity.

However, one day one of the Year Six teachers came to me looking thoroughly harassed.

"I'm really fed up with some of the girls in my class!" he declared. "They're always fighting and arguing, and I spend half my time trying to sort them out, especially after a lunch time. Could you do something, like talking to them and getting them to be nice to each other for a change?"

Oh yeah, and then I could sort out World Peace, I suppose, I felt like saying. I knew what a problem girls of that age could be because, hard as it was to believe, I had been a Year Six girl myself once, and I can remember the anguish of somebody not talking to me, and getting other girls to exclude me as well. To my shame, I can also remember joining in somebody else's exclusion plans. In fact, when the Headteacher found out about the latter he smacked us all! Children today don't know they're born!

I gave a lot of thought to what Bill had said, and decided that maybe I ought to try a Friendship Club consisting of these girls. They could meet at lunch time to discuss problems, find solutions and do activities which would unite them and stop them fighting. Well, you have to aim high, don't you?

I consulted Bill and he gave my plans an enthusiastic

welcome. At the very worst, that would be one lunch time when he wouldn't have to sort them out!

He gave me a list of the girls, only five of them, and I did proper invitations to join my new club. Bill duly gave them out and I sat back and waited to see their response.

The next day I was in my room at break time getting ready for my next lesson, when there was a knock on the door.

Two of the girls peered in.

"Miss Young, can we talk to you?" I assured them that they could always come and talk to me, and they ventured in and sat down.

"The thing is that we would like to come to your club but we don't want Tessa and Jane to come."

Right, so 40% of the club doesn't want 40% of the club to come! Great start!

"No, I'm sorry girls, but you can't make conditions like that," I said firmly. "You can't pick and choose who comes, that's up to me."

The two of them looked at each other while I held my breath, metaphorically speaking. At this rate the whole idea could fail before it had started.

"We can eat our lunch together and I'll provide drinks. We can discuss things, play games, make things - you can decide together."

The mention of food and drink obviously swayed them and they both nodded.

"OK, we'll come!"

Off they went, looking reasonably happy.

Five minutes later, there was another knock at the door.

This time Tessa and Jane looked in.

"Miss Young, can we have a word, please?"

"Ye-es," I said hesitating. This was looking familiar.

"The thing is that we want to come to your club but we don't want to come if Kayleigh and Rosie are coming!"

I felt like exploding and giving them a piece of my mind, but I realised that this would achieve nothing except a rise in my blood pressure and a headache.

I explained to them what I had already told the other two, and I was relieved when the answer came back more or less the same.

Well, at least nobody had objected to Sarah coming! In the staff room at lunch time I bent Bill's ear.

"I'm not sure that this is a good idea, Bill," I began, trying to look pathetic.

"I think it's a wonderful idea, Pam, and I can't wait for it to start!"

"Yeah, but Bill, they haven't even been yet and already they're causing trouble!"

"Exactly! This is what it's like for me all the time! Give me a break, Pam! Anyway, if you do it I'll make all your cups of tea for a week!"

Well, that did it! He must be desperate if he was promising that! It was only later that I realised that he was so hard-working that he was rarely in the staff room, so I think that I got one drink out of him!

The day came when the newly formed Friendship Club was to meet. I must admit that I was feeling distinctly wary, but determined to give it a go. I had juice and biscuits ready, and the plan included a talk with the girls about a name for the club, and agreeing with them what we were going to do each week.

"Hi, girls!" I greeted them cheerfully as they all came

171

in together. I decided to ignore the black looks that were all too obvious behind each other's backs.

"Hi, Miss Young!" they all chorused back, each one trying to look as if butter wouldn't melt in their mouths.

"Right, come and sit down." I motioned them to the chairs round the table.

Kayleigh looked at me in disbelief. "I'm not sitting next to Tessa," she stated baldly.

"Neither am I!" declared Rosie.

"Well, I'm not sitting next to you!" Tessa spat at Kayleigh.

"Girls, girls, girls!" I raised my voice just to make myself heard. "This is getting us nowhere. Look, you two," I indicated Kayleigh and Rosie. "Sit here at this side of the table, Tessa and Jane sit there, and Sarah, you sit in the middle."

Sarah had a goody two shoes look on her face but I wasn't fooled.

"And I'll sit next to Sarah," I said firmly.

I gave out the drinks and offered each girl a biscuit. Thank goodness I'd had the sense to get identical ones.

"Right, let's talk about the name of our club. What do you think to the name that I have suggested already - the Friendship Club?"

Silence reigned and sulky looks replaced the black ones. I couldn't decide which ones I preferred.

"It's alright, I suppose," was one reluctant answer.

"Yes, I suppose," was another.

"Yeah, OK," came another.

I was bowled over by their enthusiasm and had to bite back some sarcastic reply. It really was like treading on eggshells, and I wondered if the clock on the wall had stopped. Was it only five minutes since they came in? Was there really another twenty five minutes to go?

So, we decided to keep the name, and the next item on the agenda was to decide our activities.

"I'd like to play card games, like Snap," declared Sarah.

"No, I don't want to do that. I'd rather do some pattern work," replied Jane, rather too quickly.

"I'm not playing games with you, Sarah," retorted Rosie. "You cheat."

"I do not, you rat bag!"

"What about yesterday in the playground, and you had to go and tell the dinner lady it was me who cheated, and I hadn't done anything wrong!"

"Yeah, that's right." Kayleigh put in her four penny-worth.

I'd had enough already.

"Right girls, if you're going to argue like this you can all go now!"

Five pairs of surprised eyes stared at me.

"And don't come the innocent all of a sudden. I've had enough of you. I invite you to my room, I give you biscuits and drinks, offer to let you play games, and this is how you repay me! Well, if you can't be civil to each other, go and have your argument some-where else! I've got work to do. I had thought that maybe sometimes you could help me with my job, and become my assistants (Now where had that idea come from? Talk about thinking on my feet!), but obviously I need to think again. I need sensible people to help me, not people who would make

173

toddlers look grown up!"

I paused for dramatic effect, but mainly because I had run out of steam and couldn't think of anything else to say. I would just have to go back to Bill and tell him I had failed.

There was a silence and I wondered if I had gone too far.

"I don't mind helping you," Jane declared.

"Me too," responded Kayleigh.

"What could we do though?" Sarah asked.

Rosie and Tessa looked at each other and mumbled something along the same lines.

They even all managed to look vaguely human and interested!

My mind raced while I quickly thought of ways in which they could help without my having to re-do everything. Actually, once I got going, I could think of quite a few ways and each one, from sorting and filing worksheets to colouring in work cards for my pupils, elicited the same positive response.

"We could call ourselves Miss Young's Helping Club," declared Sarah and they all nodded with great enthusiasm.

I couldn't believe that this was actually happening. Not for the first time I had managed to think of something off the top of my head, and it was quite a good idea, though I said so myself!

"I could make badges for you to wear, saying that you are my assistants and," I played my trump card, "I could have some stickers made especially for you, saying what you have done to help me."

Hmm, maybe I was getting a bit carried away there, but if it would help I was willing to spend money.

At that moment the bell rang for afternoon school to start again. That twenty five minutes had gone rather quickly.

The girls went out reluctantly as they were now full of what they were going to do to justify the title 'Miss Young's Assistant', and were willing to start there and then.

I persuaded them to go, but said that I was looking forward to seeing them next Tuesday. I even thought I detected a few faint smiles as they left, but I couldn't be sure!

As soon as they had gone I sank back into my chair, exhausted. I tensed up again though as I heard a knock at my door. I relaxed as Bill put his head round the door and raised his eyebrows.

"How did you get on?" he enquired. "Do you need a lie down in a darkened room or a couple of headache tablets, or both?"

"No, just a cup of tea, Bill, and make it milky, no sugar, thanks. Believe me, this will be the first of many you owe me!"

§

Lunch times were always a problem for some pupils. Some felt isolated and alone, as they had nobody to play with. Some children were bullied, although this word covers a whole range of activities, from name-calling to physical violence. At all of the schools where I taught there was minor bullying, but nothing too drastic.

However, if you feel lonely and excluded, playtimes can be horrendous. We tried everything we could think of at all the schools, but it was a problem which was always having to be addressed.

We had playtime buddies; older children who be-friended younger children and played with them.

The midday supervisors, or dinner ladies as all the children called them, were all trained in activities they could do with the children.

PE apparatus and games were bought and the pupils shown how to use them.

We even had a lady from the Behaviour Support Team who came to show the troublesome children, and others, how to play the old-fashioned games we had all played, and which had kept us out of trouble. Some of the children were quite reluctant to come, but with rewards of stickers and certificates, we managed to keep most of them on board.

But I could honestly say that we never really got to grips with the problems of playtimes, no matter what initiative we tried. There were always fights and children complaining about other children, and some standing alone without any friends.

So, I persevered with the Drop-In Club at my next school and within a few weeks of starting there I had quite a few children coming every Tuesday lunch time, mostly those with Special Needs.

Soon after I started the club it was Easter time, so I decided that we would have an Easter party. The girls could make Easter bonnets with paper flowers, they could all make an Easter nest out of Rice Krispies and chocolate with mini eggs in them, and they could colour in patterns to make brightly coloured paper Easter eggs.

I also found some Easter wordsearches which I knew

would go down well with the boys. It was interesting that I had quite a few boys attending, as in other schools boys wouldn't have come in case the other boys called them cissies.

I duly issued invitations to any child who had been to at least one session, but word soon spread and I was inundated with children who decided to come on the spur of the moment. Hmm, I didn't think so! They were so transparent and protested their innocence quite vehemently when I questioned their motives.

It was hard work on the day of the party as I went from group to group, helping the children with the different activities. Fortunately there were some older girls there, not Special Needs children, who were really helpful.

I was staggered at one point to see the Year Six boys colouring in the paper eggs, and doing it really well. I went over and watched in amazement.

"I didn't think you would want to colour in," I said, smiling at them.

One of them looked up at me.

"Well, ever since we were really little we have never been allowed to colour anything in. There's never been any time because we always had to write something, or do something like a Science experiment or some Maths."

"Yeah," agreed his friend, "it's not so much fun now."

"Sometimes I just want to play in the sandpit or water tray like the Reception children," another sighed wistfully.

I felt both angry and sad that these children were under so much pressure, by the use of targets and testing that the government was insisting would produce a better education system. How wrong it is! Anyway, the party was a great success and other children looked on enviously as the Drop-In children left my room, clutching chocolate nests, word-searches and coloured eggs, and the girls wearing Easter bonnets. Suddenly, my Club became very popular!

Hayley was a ten year old girl who had just come from another school. She had learning problems, although not very severe ones, and she was having trouble settling in. She came to me for help with Numeracy in a group of five children.

The other problem was that she had a prominent birthmark on one side of her face, and she always thought that the other children were staring at her and making fun of her. In fact, once the children had got used to it, and they did this very quickly, they never noticed it. She was a very angry child, and would often spit out at some unfortunate classmate, "Wot you staring at then?"

Although Maths had been my subject at College, the methods employed to teach it had changed so much - well, there had been a few intervening years! - and at a school like this, the standards were so high that children who were a bit behind with their work would probably be average in another school, with one or two exceptions.

So, I was forever having to read up on the subject in the Numeracy File, or go and ask a member of Staff how they taught this particular topic. The latter was important, because at this school certain methods were used which might not have been used in another school, and uniformity was essential.

I really could have done with some more training, and I solved the problem myself by sitting in on class Numeracy Hours so that I could see how things were done.

I was really stretched when I had to teach Numeracy to ten and eleven year olds. Sometimes it was a case of, "Now, I've written this problem up on the board, so would anybody like to come and explain how to solve it?"

There would usually be someone who had remembered something from their class lesson and, with everybody chipping in their thoughts, which jogged my memory or clarified what I had been thinking, we usually arrived at the right answer!

Very occasionally I would come up with an incorrect answer.

"Miss Young, I don't think that's right! The answer should be 28, shouldn't it?"

Borrowing Captain Mainwaring's ruse I would find myself saying, "Ah, I wondered who would spot that! Well done for noticing my deliberate mistake!"

However, I would be grinning like mad and I fooled no-one. I could almost convince myself that it did the children good, because they could see that everybody makes mistakes, and that you shouldn't think that you are a loser, or that the world is going to come to an end if you get something wrong.

If ever I spilt something I would say to the children, "It doesn't matter as long as I do something about it and wipe it up quickly."

When I made a mistake - and who doesn't? - I would acknowledge it and point to a poster that I had on my wall, which read:

"It doesn't matter if you make mistakes as long as you learn from them."

For many of my children it **was** the end of the world and a major strop could follow. This was the trouble with Hayley. In the group of five she felt threatened by what she saw as their superior knowledge, and her inadequacy came out as bad behaviour.

She would come into the lesson reasonably OK but after a few minutes you could see her face begin to darken, then a scowl would develop, then the cry of, "I ain't doing this! It's stupid! Wot you staring at?" would echo round the room as the other children stared at her.

Then they would stare at me, as if to say, What are you going to do about this then, Miss Young?

She would start to prowl around the room looking daggers at everybody, and woe betide any child who laughed at her!

Sometimes she would just slump into a chair in a corner of the room, and I'm afraid that all I could do was leave her there until the end of the lesson, as I had the other four children to consider.

Really, she needed one to one teaching, but this just wasn't possible.

I began to dread the Maths lessons with Hayley. Her attendance at school wasn't brilliant and, although I couldn't condone this, it was a relief when she didn't come to the lessons.

I needed to bolster her self-esteem but I couldn't do that in the Numeracy lessons. Although she was the poorest in the group, I suggested to her teacher that she didn't come anymore. I was well aware that it looked as if I was abdicating all responsibility for her, but the sessions were making her feel inferior, the other children were suffering because of the disruption to the lessons, and I was certainly suffering as well! So, what to do with her instead?

I knew that Hayley was quite artistic and loved to make things, especially cards. It is a truism that every child is good at something, and if you can find that something, and sometimes I admit, it's not easy, then you can build on that and their self-esteem can grow. Hayley also had relationship problems with the other girls, and could often fly off the handle at them. There was often an issue with groups of girls in the playground who were at loggerheads with each other, and Hayley was usually at the centre of things. So, if I could persuade her to come to my Drop-In Club, we could kill two birds with one stone. We could start to make greetings cards, which she would enjoy, it would take her explosive behaviour away from the playground, and maybe peace would return.

The next time that the group met, I put the idea of making greetings cards to the children. My plan was to set up a 'business', make the cards really professionally, and then sell them to the children and Staff. I asked for their thoughts and opinions and was delighted by their enthusiasm.

"Yeah, cool, let's make lots of money!"

"You mean we could really sell something that we've made!"

"My mum would buy some. She's always buying cards!"

"Yeah, but hang on, where do we get the stuff to make the cards? They would have to look like ones that you see in the shops!"

I was ready for that one.

"Well, if we're going to do it properly as a business, my husband and I will lend you some money, that's called a loan, and you can pay us back as the money comes in. Then we can buy the materials from craft shops, as well as using things we may already have."

The children's eyes widened.

"You will also need a treasurer, that's somebody who looks after the money, pays the bills and tells us how much money we've got."

The children's eyes opened even wider.

"So, if we make lots of money we can all have a share and I can buy a game for my computer!" one bright spark declared.

"And I could have a new bike then!" chipped in another.

"Hang on, hang on," I hurriedly leapt in. "I doubt that we'll make a huge profit, but if we did make any money I thought that we could give it to a charity, after you've paid us our loan back."

An air of despondency filled the room.

"I tell you what, we'll have a party to celebrate our first sales!" I encouraged them.

It worked!

"Oh, yes, brilliant!"

"When can we start?"

"When's the party?"

"Can we give the money to the RSPCA?"

"What's the RSP.......whatever?"

"Bags I look after the money!"

No way, I already had a very mature sensible girl earmarked for that job.

"My Mum makes cards, and I think that she'll come

and show us what to do and give us some stuff."

Now that sounded very interesting and we all turned with interest to look at Michael, whose pronouncement had shut everyone else up.

After school that day I rang his Mum up and told her what he had said. She said she would be delighted to come to school to show us what she did, and not only would she give us some card and accessories, but she would lend us some stamps and little devices to cut out shapes.

She was as good as her word and her first session with the children inspired us all. She was a very nice lady, and we sat for ages after the children had gone back to their classes, putting the world to rights and sympathising with each other about our own mothers who were both very unwell.

She lent or gave us a great deal of materials, and I shall always be grateful to her for her generosity and enthusiasm. The children and I were all really sad when the family moved to Gloucestershire, but we made them a very nice card which we all signed! I think they appreciated it.

As word spread about our card-making business other people gave us materials as well, or said that they would buy the cards. This was before they had even seen them!

To get back to Hayley. As the children all sat around the tables designing their cards, after a brief reminder about the materials available and the sort of cards we were going to make, I was aware that Hayley was in her element.

Because the cards had to be of a very high standard if we were going to sell them to the public, I wouldn't let anybody stick anything on a card until I had seen it and vetted it.

At the beginning of every session, after a quick reminder of what they were going to do, I would always remind the children about the golden rule.

"We know, Miss Young!" they would say. Then they would chant in unison, "Don't stick anything on until you've shown it to Miss Young!"

All edges had to be straight and it should be perfect when they had finished. There were to be no cries of, "Oh, it'll do!"

Hayley not only had some good and original designs, but she executed them really well, and when she came to me for her work to be vetted I knew that I wouldn't have to change a thing.

I praised her and then began suggesting that if other children were stuck, or I had a long line of children waiting to see me, then they could go to Hayley. This was a huge help as I really had to work hard in these sessions, as it seemed everybody wanted me all the time.

We had sheets of joined up letters saying 'Happy Birthday' or 'Thank You' or some other greeting which were a devil to peel off and then a devil to put on straight on the card. This was no problem for Hayley and, whereas I could take ages to do it, and other children couldn't do it at all, Hayley was extremely efficient.

Soon the children would by-pass me, as I usually had a long queue, and go straight to Hayley, which suited me and suited them as she was quicker. This helped Hayley to grow in confidence even more and was a huge help to me.

Her behaviour was exemplary and she was patient and kind with the other children. At the end of the session, although I had insisted that the children all tidied up for me, she would stay behind, with another girl, and finish off. She was a different girl to the unhappy, disruptive child who had once been such a problem in the Maths lessons, and our relationship benefited as well.

She started to drop in to see me at playtimes and lunch times and although it sometimes wasn't convenient, and I wondered if she was just coming in out of the cold, I was glad that we had such a good relationship now.

She would do little jobs for me and seemed to be more relaxed and happier. The other teachers could see a slight improvement too, although in the class room, when she had trouble keeping up with the other children, she could still 'lose it'.

The day came when we had forty cards all bagged and ready to be sold. A very kind lady who helped us by hearing the poorer readers in the Infants had made us some stickers to go on the backs of the cards.

They read: 'Handmade by the children of the Drop-In Club', and the children thought that they were lovely as they proudly stuck them on their cards.

We decided to sell them at break times and lunch time on one particular day in my room. Soon after the doors opened we were inundated by Staff and pupils alike. The children had done their own publicity, under my guidance, and it had worked! By the end of the day we had sold out and made £40! Well, a little more, in fact, as many of the very generous Staff hadn't claimed their change, saying that we could buy more materials with it.

Even Educational Professionals visiting the school that day had come to do their bit, and of course everybody had commented on the beautifully made cards and the confidence and good manners of the children who ran the stall. Little did they realise how much preparation had gone into the smooth running of that day, and how the children had been coached in what to say and how to say it! I had left no stone unturned!

The children were thrilled at their success and were eager to replenish stocks, but I insisted first that we had a meeting to discuss what we were going to do with the money. The upshot was that they paid my husband and I half of what we loaned them ie £15, £10 went to charity and the rest on more materials. These children were rapidly learning about business, albeit on a small scale, and I was very proud of them. As Christmas was fast approaching, we decided to make Christmas cards next, and soon Tuesday lunch times were busily spent making trees, baubles, presents, Santas, and Rudolphs to decorate our cards. Hayley was again in her element, but there was another child who came into his own and really made a great contribution to our business.

Neil was a lovely boy but was, shall we say, lively, and in class he could be a problem. We had a good relationship and in a small group he was manageable. He was Dyslexic, so he really struggled with reading, writing and spelling. Like Hayley, he was artistic and was especially good at making 3-D pictures and models.

One day a lady asked to speak to me on the 'phone.

It turned out that she lived in the village, had heard about our card-making business, and wondered if I would like to borrow her Sisix machine on a long term loan.

I thanked her very much, said that we would love to, and arranged for her to bring it to school.

I put the 'phone down and turned to the other members of Staff.

"Does anybody know what a Sisix machine is?" I enquired.

Yes, I know I should have admitted my ignorance on the 'phone, but I hadn't, and nobody in the room had the slightest idea either.

"You'll just have to see what turns up," declared the Head, grinning, "and let's hope it's something you want. That serves you right for not admitting you didn't have a clue what she was talking about!"

The machine duly came, and with it various stamps that you fitted into it to make different shapes. It wasn't quite as easy as that though. For example, if you wanted to do a Santa face you had to stamp out a hat in red, his beard, eyebrows and part of the hat in white and his face in pink. Never being very good with mechanical things, I could feel my eyes glazing over as the lady talked me through the complicated instructions.

Thank goodness, as she did so, Neil was hovering nearby. In a flash of inspiration I called him over.

"Neil, come and listen to this and then you can be in charge of it."

He came willingly and listened intently to all the instructions. He even managed to ask all the right questions and he soon beamed confidently at the lady. She was probably thinking something along the lines of, what kind of teacher is this who can't understand simple instructions and has to hand over to one of her pupils?

At every session Neil would stand at the machine, patiently stamping out shapes the other children would request. It was not an easy job, either, as you had to be very precise and careful to get everything lined up just so.

He would concentrate hard for half an hour at a time, a record for most children his age, and definitely a huge achievement for him. Eventually he asked me if he could train another boy to be his assistant as he couldn't keep up with the demand!

When the Headteacher came in one day to see what the famous Sisix machine did, I just referred him to Neil, who explained it to him much better than I could have done!

The children decided they would sell their cards at the Christmas Fair organised by the parents at the beginning of December. Preparations were going well until I realised that the Friday night it was to be held coincided with a weekend away my husband had arranged for my birthday.

Hmm, now what were we going to do about that? I wasn't going to give up my romantic weekend away! Fortunately, some of the mums said they would keep an eye on the children who wanted to run the stall, and as I instructed them on what they had to do (and wrote everything down as well), I reckoned that they would be alright.

Much to their delight they sold out again and our coffers were swelled by the amazing amount of £35!

A board meeting was hastily arranged and ideas on how to spend the money were debated. In the end they decided to pay off the rest of their loan, give £10 to charity and the rest was to spend on materials.

Valentine cards were the next on our list and soon we had many different variations on the theme of love. Amazingly, the boys were quite happy about making these!

By now, members of Staff were coming to us as they would to a card shop, and even Tony, our visiting Educational Psychologist, would buy his wife's birthday card and Valentine card from us.

Eventually, as is the way with most childhood enthusiasms, the children's interest began to wane. The Summer term seemed a good time to wind up the business, when many of the older children would be leaving to go on to their Secondary School. After all, we could always start it up again if the children wanted to go down that route.

By now, we had a very good reputation for raising money and I was keen for that to continue.

We had discovered a company called World Vision which encouraged you to buy gifts for people in the Third World. You know the sort of thing - seeds for a family farm costs £9, eighteen fruit trees cost £16, five chickens cost £4, and so on. This idea appealed to the children, as they could see what their money was being spent on, instead of just giving a donation to a charity.

We had many discussions about what they wanted to buy. At first they refused to buy any livestock as they were sure they would be eaten. I patiently explained to them that the animals would be used for breeding (not in too much detail though. I never did teach sex education and thank goodness for that!), and they soon recognised that you didn't just give the poor people food.

You had to give them something that would enable them to feed themselves, and be sustainable in the future. The children learnt this remarkably quickly and soon gained more of an insight into helping others.

They weren't too keen on buying school-based items either eg lessons for five children cost £12.

"Cor, who wants to go to school if you don't have to?"

"I'd pay £12 not to have lessons!"

"Yeah, no school - what a great idea!"

So we had a whole session devoted to discussing the value of education, and what would happen if none of them ever went to school again. They listened carefully and I think they realised, although grudgingly, how the Third World families were desperate for their children to be educated to get themselves out of poverty. The children 'out there' thought that it was a privilege to go to school and they were so proud of their uniforms and equipment.

I should imagine that their Lost Property box, indeed if they had one, was usually empty, while ours was usually overflowing, and often with really valuable items like coats. I'm sure our throwaway society sends out the wrong signals. If a child loses something, it's not a problem because the parents just buy another one. This is not true for all families, of course, but it is for many.

I knew I was getting through to some of the children

when, during one of our heated discussions, someone poured scorn on the idea of being pleased to own a plastic bucket.

"But a plastic bucket would be really precious to them and they would treasure it!" replied Rachel.

The other children nodded in agreement and the boy who made the original remark had the grace to look ashamed.

I think some of the children recognised that we in our country have so many possessions, while many in the world had hardly any, but that this does not make us any happier. In fact possessions, and the obtaining of them, can make us very unhappy.

If you mentioned the word 'love' many of the boys would groan and mime being sick, but I think it was important to say that love, education, friendship, and so on are far more valuable. And if any parents objected to my philosophy on life, then I really didn't care.

It would say more about them if they complained, and I would quite happily have defended my corner. It would be easy to think that surely nobody could object to these views but, believe me, free speech from teachers was not always possible.

Having said that, I once had a parent who thanked me on Parents' Night for making such a difference to her daughter's view on life. Apparently, in her reading book there had been a picture of a race on Sports Day, and I had commented that the important thing in a race was to do your best and finish. Winning was desirable but not the be-all and end-all. To her non-sporty daughter this had been a revelation, and she could see that it applied to other areas of life too.

In this job you never knew when you could make a difference by a chance remark. You never knew when you were offending by a chance remark too!

So, our fund raising activities from then on centred on the World Vision catalogue, and I had to order many more so that the children could spend ages poring over them.

One day, Ruby came to me with £4 in her hand.

"It was my birthday yesterday and I got some money given to me. Please will you order me some chickens for the African families?"

I looked at her and smiled, trying to keep the emotion I was feeling out of my voice.

"Are you really sure about this and does Mum know?"

"Oh yes, she knows and it's fine with her."

"Ruby, I'm really proud of you and I bet your parents are too."

She grinned at me.

"Well, if you could order them for me please." She turned to walk away.

"I've had a better idea. Would you like to do it on the 'phone? I'll help you."

She looked thrilled and said, "Could I really?"

I made the 'phone call, explaining to the person who answered that Ruby would like to say what she wanted, and I paid with my debit card. It took a while to explain that I wasn't just pocketing her £4 as I put the coins in my pocket!

When the new school year started, the Club had some of the old stalwarts and a handful of newcomers attending, but as the weeks went by and word spread, we soon built up our numbers again.

After a few weeks of playing games and doing Craft

activities, I broached the subject of running an event to raise money for World Vision. The children were, as ever, very enthusiastic, and the ideas came thick and fast.

"Could we have a Summer Fair, like the parents organise?"

(What, in the middle of November? Besides, that idea had been tried and, I must say, it was one of the most traumatic lunch times I had ever spent, so that was a definite no-no.)

"Could we all bring our pets to school and have a pet show?"

"Ooh yes, and we could have dog races and rabbit races and mouse races and…"

"Stop!" I hurriedly shouted amidst the generally positive comments these ideas were generating.

"I'm sorry, but we can't have lots of animals in school for just half an hour at lunch time!"

The children looked downcast and amid cries of, "Why not?" and "Aw!" I tried to reason with them and point out the snags in this plan. Actually, not being an animal lover, I never thought that I would hear myself say this, but thank heavens for Health and Safety regulations!

The children accepted my reasoning, but were not downcast for long.

"What about a Bring and Buy Sale?"

"Yes, we could all bring our toys that we don't want any more."

"Yeah, my Mum's always on at me to clear out my room!"

"We'll have to have it in a bigger room, Mrs Young's room isn't big enough!"

The surge of enthusiasm grew bigger and bigger and I must admit that, although I wanted them to think about the implications of their plan and so consider the snags, I was beginning to wonder if perhaps this plan would work.

I looked at the clock.

"It's one o'clock and time to go, but I promise I will talk to the Headteacher and see what he thinks."

The children appeared to be quite happy with that and went back to their classes seemingly mollified.

The Headteacher had no objections to a Bring and Buy Sale so a date was fixed and plans started to be made.

I wanted the children to be involved with every step of the organisation, and I saw my role as being that of a facilitator, asking questions of them and checking that they had thought of everything.

The first snag was that my room wasn't big enough, so where were we to find a room which was large enough and not being used for anything else? This is a perennial problem in any school and one that I have touched on before. We realised that the three Infant classes were going out for the day on an educational visit, so we could have one of their rooms, as long as we left it exactly as we found it. The room was also one of two that this particular class had, so when they came back to school to collect their belongings they could use the other room.

Publicity was the next item to be considered and we all decided that posters done on the computer looked much more professional than handmade ones. I had to admit to a small problem though.

"If you want to do the posters on the computer, and

I think that you should, you will have to do them by yourselves because you all know more about the different computer programs than I do!"

The children reassured me, quite solicitously, that they would be fine. In fact they went further.

"Would you like us to show you what to do, Mrs Young?"

"I could teach you anything you don't know!" (You haven't got enough time!)

"You don't need to come with us even, because we'll be alright!"

(There was the small matter of them being unsupervised to consider here.)

So we all trooped off to the Computer Suite and they settled down to work while I got my sandwich out - well, I had to eat it sometime! They were doing really well, only asking for the occasional spellings, when suddenly all the screens went blank for no apparent reason. I swore under my breath - although sometimes in extreme conditions I had often felt like swearing, I never uttered a rude word in front of the children - and went over to them trying to look intelligent. The children, having got over their initial shock, looked philosophical about it, and resigned themselves to starting again.

This is one of the problems when the computers are on a network - what one does they all do.

The other problem was that the children hadn't saved anything as they went on, so at very short-spaced intervals I would call out, "Save your work!"

This seemed to be working until Catherine let out a howl and shouted, "I've lost my writing!"

As one we all shouted to each other, "Save!"

Oh, the joy of computers! Don't get me wrong, when they work they are an invaluable tool, but when they go wrong they are the most time-consuming and frustrating, stress-inducing things around.

Eventually, when the time for them to go back into class had been and gone, ("Just apologise to your teacher and say that I had trouble with the computers - they will understand!") we had ten pretty good posters which I soon put up on various walls round the school.

My room soon started to look like a store room for a charity shop. I could hardly move for boxes and bags as the children and parents very generously scoured their homes for things we could sell.

Carla staggered into school one day dragging a huge black bin liner filled with what looked like most of her possessions. I peered into it and was staggered by her generosity.

"Are you quite sure that you want to part with all these things, Carla? You can't have got much left!"

She looked me in the eye and said firmly, "If it will help the poor children then that's alright!"

That was me put in my place then!

When the day of the sale came, Carla came rushing into the room with her purse ready and headed for the stall for small toys, most of the items having been provided by her.

I couldn't believe it when she started buying half the stall, including many things that I was sure that she had brought herself. She was actually buying back her own toys! I sidled up to her and said quietly, "Carla, you don't have to pay for your own toys. If you want them back just take them."

She looked up at me from her height of four feet nothing and said with as much dignity as she could muster, "This money is for the poor children and I want to help them."

I felt about two feet tall.

"Well done, Carla," I managed to blurt out. "I'm very proud of you."

I wondered what her Mum would say when she went home with all the stuff that she had brought, and minus a fair amount of money. I made a mental note to ring her Mum up and explain what Carla had done. Her Mum was lovely and also very proud of her daughter.

To go back a few hours, it was obviously up to me to set everything up as the teachers who had volunteered to help me at the actual sale, and all the children, were busily occupied in their classes.

I drew a plan of the classroom where we were to have the sale, marking the position of all the furniture and the equipment on it. That took me a while for a start! Val, one of the teachers, had said there was some stuff for the sale in her classroom, but as she had gone on the trip I couldn't ask her if I had got the right bags. I peered into them and thought that it was just the sort of things we needed, so I carted them off and set them out on the stalls.

I must admit that time was tight and I had to go and teach so the last few things were virtually thrown onto the stall. Why was it so difficult to price everything? I was doubting my own ability to get the prices just right, and I could have done with some expert advice. I mean, this pair of shoes looked like new and there was a name in them as well. Oh heck, the penny dropped, and I hastily looked on the floor for the bag that they had come out of, realising that I must have picked up the wrong bag and nearly sold somebody's shoes! In their haste to be off on the trip the child must have put their shoes on the nearest pile, not aware that I was going to be coming along collecting as much stuff as I could find!

Val had a good laugh when I told her I had nearly sold a pair of new shoes belonging to one of her children! (It turned out that many of the children had changed into their wellies to go on the trip as the weather had been very wet.)

We also had a cake stall that I and many of the parents and Staff had been baking for, and I had brought quite a few pairs of earrings which my husband and I had made in our jewellery business from way back when. If I sold one pair, I thought, it will be something, and at 50p a pair they were priced to go.

In fact I think that we sold seventeen pairs and I rather wished that we had priced them a bit higher!

At half past three we were all waiting expectantly for the crowds to surge in. At twenty to four we were still waiting and I was beginning to get worried.

Two of the girls asked if they could go out into the playground and remind the parents and children. We had lots of signs all around school and outside, but I thought that anything was worth a try. Well, I did, until a parent came in to complain that the girls' attitude and language were **very** persuasive. I tried to explain how they wanted to raise as much money as possible for poor people, but I called the children in as well.

By a quarter to four a few people had come and, because of their generosity, we had at least made some money. Cake stalls usually do very well at this sort of event, but even there business was slow. The buns and small cakes were going very well, but only because the children on the stalls were buying them! Ah well, by this time I was beginning to think that I was going to have to do some explaining to my husband that night as I staggered home with the contents of most of the stalls and no money in my purse, so I didn't care who bought anything.

Eventually the room was quite crowded and trade was fairly brisk, so my worries were eased slightly.

It's always interesting watching children browse at something like this, and it was often impossible to predict what they were going to buy. Paul told me that he was looking for a birthday present for his Dad. Now, Paul had definite Special Needs and, how shall I put this tactfully, his Dad wasn't the brightest button in the box, so I was alarmed to see that Paul had chosen a book entitled 'A History of Philosophy'!

"I'm not sure that your Dad would enjoy that one," I said as tactfully as I could.

"Oh, he likes reading," declared Paul, clutching the book tightly.

"This one looks interesting," I persisted, holding up a rather battered Wilbur Smith novel.

I could see why he had gone for the philosophy book; it had a shiny leatherette and gold cover and looked most attractive.

"Nah, I think that he will like this one," he replied firmly and I had to give in. Well, it's the thought that counts!

By now I was beginning to flag, and I was very grateful to the members of Staff and the parents who had come to help us. At half past four we started to pack away, and I was not feeling optimistic about the amount of money that we had made. The children had confided in me that they wanted to raise £100 at least, and I was not looking forward to seeing their faces when they realised that their target had not been made.

At least all the cakes had gone, thanks to a mum who had come later on and, realising we were desperate to get rid of the last few, had bought them all. I never cease to be amazed by people's generosity. Quite a few members of Staff had been unable to come so had sent very generous donations.

Ruth's Mum, who had been helping me to run things, took one look at my strained face and said, "Would you like me to load all the stuff that's left into my car and I'll take it all to the local charity shop?"

I was so grateful that I could have kissed her, and it gave me the chance to start counting the money, as the children were desperate to know how much we had made. I kept on making pessimistic noises about the possible amount, as I really didn't want them to be disappointed.

While the children helped her to load the car, some tried to follow my plan of the classroom so that we could put everything back in the right place. (It helped to have the plan the right way up!)

As I looked at the pile of notes and coins I felt rather more optimistic that we might have made more than I thought, but £100 - no, not a chance!

In fact we had made £125! I still have no idea how

we did it, but the delight on the children's faces as they danced around the room celebrating was a joy to behold.

They had been hoping to raise enough money to buy a pig for a family. Now they could do that and more. It had all been worthwhile and we all went home weary but happy. I still wonder what Paul's Dad made of his birthday present though!

§

A much easier way of making money was to take a basic foodstuff, like potatoes, add value to them, and then sell the finished article to the Staff. School Staff are always hungry and will eat most things. Anyone on a diet has no chance in a staff room, as there are always biscuits and cakes galore when somebody celebrates a birthday, or grateful parents show their appreciation by sending in a box of chocolates or something equally delicious.

So the children and I decided that we would cook jacket potatoes and serve them, with fillings, to the Staff one lunch time.

As we sat down one day to plan the event I was determined that the children should organise as much as possible.

Yes, they would scrub the potatoes the day before. This we did and, when they went back to their classes, I scrubbed each one again! Well, I wanted everything to be just right and I didn't want the children serving up dirty food!

I pointed to the tiny Baby Belling oven which is what we used for cooking and which was very, well, basic is the word that springs to mind.

"So how are we going to cook thirty jacket potatoes in there?"

Their enthusiasm was infectious and could not be dented, and rightly so, but I wanted them to think of every eventuality and to plan every detail.

"I think that we can get them all in there!" one bright spark declared.

I silently opened the oven door (the oven wasn't on, I hasten to add), and produced a bag of potatoes, having anticipated such a remark.

"OK, you see how many you can get in there."

The bright spark seized the bag and started cramming in as many potatoes as he could. When he got to ten he had to admit defeat. He couldn't squeeze another one in **and** shut the door.

The children all shared his disappointment.

"That's OK. There is another answer," I quickly reassured them.

"Think where there is another oven in school."

Eventually the penny dropped.

"The school kitchen where they cook our dinners!"

"Yes, that's right, so who is going to ask the School Cook if we can borrow her oven?"

Of course I had already talked to her about it so she was expecting the children to come, although I had asked her to look surprised!

Two of the children volunteered and jumped up to go right there and then.

"Yes, well, I think we ought to wait until the end of lunch time as she might just be a bit busy at the moment!"

So, our lovely Cook and her helper duly agreed to

cook all the potatoes for us, and we then had to decide what fillings to make. As before, the children made posters to advertise the event and a menu, so that we could take orders before the day, and would know exactly how much food to prepare.

I had taught the children that if you ask for donations for something like this you will probably make more money as people are usually very generous, and I knew that our Staff would be no exception.

The day before our cafe, as they were all very enthusiastically scrubbing the potatoes and I was trying to keep the floor reasonably dry, I said, "Right, tonight, on the way home from school, I will go and buy all the other ingredients. Has anybody got any money I can take with me?"

The children looked up from their 'let's see how much water we can use to scrub a potato' activities and gazed at me in bewilderment.

"I've got some money at home," a few said willingly.

"But I need it now really."

Silence.

I took pity on them.

"How about if I use my own money and then you can repay me from the money that you make tomorrow?"

I could tell from the doubtful looks that they hadn't thought about this, and really they wanted all the money we made to go to children in Third World countries.

"So you think it would be alright for me to spend the money I was going to use to buy food for my husband on this food for the Staff?"

I pointed out that I had already donated one bag of potatoes which I had brought from home.

The children reluctantly agreed that maybe it wouldn't be fair to spend my money on the ingredients, and they agreed that my plan was the right one. I felt it was important that they learn how things work in the big wide world, and if they were disappointed then they would have to get over it. What a hard woman!

I wouldn't change my mind and when I gave them the receipt the next day they paid up willingly, though I suspect they had asked their parents if this was how things worked.

That morning break they all converged on my room, and we moved tables, checked orders, set out thirty sets of cutlery wrapped in paper serviettes, grated cheese, plated up thirty portions of salad and mixed all the other fillings.

It was a bit of a rush but we managed to do most of it. I finished it myself later, then just before noon I collected the potatoes. The Cooks had been brilliant and thirty potatoes were cooked perfectly. I made sure that the children wrote little notes of thanks later, and I bought some flowers for them.

At lunch time my room was soon full of excited children, but before they did anything I sent them to wash their hands. Some of them opened their mouths to say that their hands were clean, but one stern look from me and they shot off to the toilets.

Of course, the trick in this situation was to look carefully at their hands when they came back. They were too excited to dry them properly, so anybody's hands that were bone dry were sent back again!

"And this time use some soap! It's that white stuff on the sink!" I responded firmly!

As soon as the Staff came in for their pre-ordered jacket potatoes the children all went very quiet and shy, and became unrecognisable as my normally noisy, bubbly enthusiastic helpers!

I had to push them into consulting their list, fetching a potato from me, (Health and Safety meant that they were forbidden from touching the oven, especially as there were so many of them! Keeping an eye on them all was wearing me out!) then spooning the relevant filling onto the opened potato.

The Staff were very patient and, as their confidence grew, the children managed on their own. And re-member that many of these children had Special Needs!

At last all the meals had been served and the children gratefully had theirs.

"How much have we made?" was a frequent cry and two of the older children sat down to count the money. After I had checked it, we took out the money owed to me and we still had £100!

The children and I were over the moon, and the World Vision catalogues soon came out as they tried to decide what to buy. All too soon it was one o'clock and the children had to go back to their classes, tired but very gratified.

So who did the washing up then? I'll give you three guesses!

16

Darts And Dominoes

The boy threw himself into a chair and smirked at me. "I don't like you," he snarled, then sagged visibly as if he had been waiting to get that off his chest for some time.

I wouldn't care, but I had only just collected him from his classroom for his first ever session with me, so he had only known me for about three minutes, and on such a short acquaintanceship he was doing a very good character assassination job. Well, if I had thought that this one was going to be easy, I was sadly mistaken.

Thoughts of taking him straight back to his class room loomed large and for two pins I would have given up there and then, but curiosity came over me, as did the thought of my pay cheque. Well, the car had just had its service and Christmas was rapidly approaching.

"So why don't you like me, then?" I enquired, with genuine interest.

"Because you're a flipping teacher, ain't you?"

I admitted that I was. Obviously there was nothing wrong with his powers of observation!

"And teachers shout at you, and nag you, and make you do fings and I'm fed up of 'em."

Resisting the urge to say, "No, don't mince your words, just say what you think," I instead took a long, hard look at the boy and said, "But I'm here to help you. I'm not going to shout, or nag you. I don't like people nagging or shouting at me, so I don't do it to others."

"Huh," came the reply, but he wisely left it at that.

Hmm, no pressure here then. Why had I agreed to take him on?

Yeah, I know - I like a challenge and the pay cheque... Oh dear, I must stop being so mercenary.

As Brian, as he was called, stared at the opposite wall I covertly appraised him.

He was a thin boy, of medium height, with a shock of bright ginger hair. He had a world-weary manner that was too old for his nine short years on earth. He could have won an Olympic gold medal for scowling and being 'bolshie', but I hoped this was all an act and that, as I suspected, there was a frightened little boy underneath who was using all this bluster to cover up his low self-esteem and unhappiness.

I had been asked to help him with his Numeracy skills which were pretty inadequate. This was unusual in a boy as - sweeping statement coming up - on the whole a nine year old boy who could read, albeit not brilliantly but well enough to manage, would usually be expected to be reasonably good at numbers. In fact he was at the level of a six year old and his behaviour was deteriorating by the hour.

No wonder his Class Teacher had greeted me so warmly when I went to collect him. The thought of being without him, and the class being able to work without his constant interruptions, must have kept her going throughout the morning.

"Would you like me to help you?"

I fired the question at him out of the blue, hoping to take him by surprise.

To be honest, I was buying time as I tried to work out my strategy.

He stared at me out of cynical eyes.

207

"Huh, you can't help me, nobody can!"

Listen, I wanted to say, I've got certificates and diplomas, experience and bloody-mindedness coming out of my ears, and I don't give up easily, so pack it in.

However, I resisted the urge, and smiled.

"Do you like football?"

This change of tack seemed to throw him.

"Yeah," he reluctantly agreed.

"Who do you support, then?"

"Man U," he replied, looking very, very slightly interested.

Oh no, I thought, not another one. Why did nobody support York City? Every child in every school seemed to support Manchester United. A little originality wouldn't come amiss!

"Do you like to watch the football on television, Brian?"

"Yeah."

Oh, this was like pulling teeth but I persevered.

"Do you watch any other sport?"

"Yeah, darts, sometimes, when it's on."

Bullseye! An idea was forming in my head and I could see the light at the end of the tunnel, and I didn't think that it was an oncoming train.

"Tell me a bit about yourself, your family, what you like to eat, anything."

Gradually he opened up a little and I found out a bit more about him. It was a familiar story. Mum was a single parent with three other boys, all with different fathers. He told me that last bit in a matter of fact way, as if it were the norm.

He didn't know where his Dad was and he said that

he didn't care, which meant that he did.

He hated school, he hated all teachers and he was fed up. My guess was that he must have had a very unsympathetic teacher at some stage, and his very obvious resentment stemmed from some unhappy experiences.

I looked at my watch. Goodness, I had been so engrossed with Brian that I had forgotten the time and he should have been back in his class at least five minutes ago. Still, I didn't think that his teacher would mind.

"It's time to go, Brian," I said, expecting him to want to get away from me.

He didn't stir.

"Do I 'ave to go back? Couldn't I stay 'til dinner time?"

You could have knocked me down with a feather!

"So, it's not been too bad then?" I asked him with a smile.

"Well, you 'aven't shouted at me."

"Or nagged you," I laughed.

A ghost of a smile appeared on his lips.

I got up and prepared to walk him back to his class room. As we went down the corridor he assumed his belligerent manner, swaggering along and scowling at everyone. As I knocked on his classroom door and turned to usher him in, I felt a tug at my sleeve and heard an urgent whisper.

"Are you coming back tomorrow?"

"Oh, yes," I reassured him, "I'll be back tomorrow."

The next day I persuaded one of the Infant Teachers to lend me a dartboard and a set of darts that she had in her Numeracy equipment.

The board was covered in a Velcro-like material and the darts were plastic with Velcro on their tips. (Now, you didn't think that they were real darts, did you?!) Brian came out of his class reasonably willingly, but the swagger was still there as we walked the few yards to my room.

"Fancy a game of darts, Brian?" I asked as I opened the door.

He frowned and looked taken aback.

"I said, do you fancy a game of darts, Brian?"

"Yeah," he said wildly, as he looked round the room for a dartboard.

His eyes fell on the plastic darts and fabric-covered dartboard.

"Them's for kids," he declared, looking none too pleased.

"Well, they're the only ones we've got so if you want a game it's those or nothing."

I held my breath as I waited for him to throw a paddy. Fortunately, after a few seconds of indecision he made up his mind.

"Yeah, alright then, I suppose so."

Right, don't overdo the enthusiasm, I felt like saying, but managed to curb my tongue.

The next hurdle for me to overcome was to hit the dartboard, but sometimes I don't mind being unable to do something in front of the children. Brian's first dart stuck on the board, while mine just managed to miss. It landed in the corner of the room and I mouthed a silent 'thank you' heavenwards as I bent to retrieve it.

His next dart missed but, although he glowered at it, there was no other reaction.

My second dart hit the board and stuck there, as did Brian's third one. My final one hit the board then slid off onto the carpet. And I had been trying!

"Right, let's add up our scores. Shouldn't take **me** long!" I smiled.

Brian frowned and I knew what was coming.

"I can't be bothered," he said and threw himself onto the chair. (That poor chair!)

"Let's have a look," I said, ignoring him. "You've got a four and a two." I held my fingers out. "So, that would be four, five, six. Well done, Brian. You're in the lead. I've got three."

I picked up the darts and held them out to him, hardly daring to breathe in case he threw them back at me. He hesitated, then took them from me and aimed at the board. Phew!

I still had to do the adding up of our scores each time, but I was patient and the main aim of that day was to involve Brian, and for him to enjoy himself.

That day he returned to his classroom with a sticker on his jumper and a hint of a smile on his face. Let's not go too far, now, Brian and crack a smile!

I felt he had regained a modicum of self-esteem and could look his classmates in the eye when he returned. I knew he would continue to have his ups and downs, but I felt that we had turned a corner in our relationship, and there was hope for him.

The next day the same old glower was there, but he had just suffered the indignity of a Numeracy Hour, when he couldn't keep up with the other children.

He was eager to get to my room though and picked up the darts, expecting the last few days' routine to continue.

When he retrieved his darts after his first throws, I took a deep breath and said to him, "I would like you to add up your score today, but you can use your fingers and I will help you."

Instead of giving him the chance to throw a 'wobbly', I carried straight on.

"So, let's see. A three and a one. Use your fingers. Put three up on one hand and one on the other. Now how many fingers can you count?"

To his surprise and my relief he found himself saying, "Four."

"Great. Now add another one."

"Five," came the answer.

Oh, yes, I thought, that has made my day. Special Needs teaching is made up of so many little triumphs like this.

He looked quite surprised but pleased, and the rest of the lesson went smoothly.

After five days of playing darts and even recording our scores, I felt that we ought to move on. That was a bit of a shame really as it was making my lesson planning incredibly easy, and I could certainly justify my methods, even to OFSTED, but we couldn't play darts forever.

So the next week I arrived with a game of dominoes. Not much difference there, I can hear you say, but the important thing to remember about nearly all SEN children is that they hate change. If Brian was expecting to play darts, and he felt safe with that, how would he react to this change, or as he would see it, this catastrophe?

The scowl reappeared and he picked up the box of dominoes and hurled it across the room.

He waited for me to react.

I was prepared, though, and took another box out of my bag. That caught him off guard!

Before he had time to pick it up, I started to stand all the dominoes up on end in a wavy line, so that when I knocked the first one down, all the others would follow.

I could see him trying to see what I was doing, without actually showing any interest.

What on earth was this crazy woman doing?

When I knocked the first one over and the others followed, he could not curb his curiosity and he turned round to look.

"Do you want to help me do another one?" I asked.

He nodded.

I then took a big risk, but one I felt that I had to take. I couldn't let him get away with throwing a box across the room.

"Then you need to pick up those dominoes, Brian."

He shook his head.

"I'll help you, but you need to do that for me."

Notice the way I didn't demand that he did it, nor did I plead. I just stated what he needed to do.

I went over to the dominoes and picked one up to show him that I would help. Thank goodness, he came over and picked one up, then another and another. I meanwhile pretended to be doing something with the box, so that he eventually found himself picking most of them up. Yes!

"Well done," I said quietly. It had been a big effort for him and I wanted to give him that recognition.

He knew that he wouldn't get a sticker because his behaviour had been awful, but he had pulled himself round and we carried on playing with the dominoes. It was a small step, but an important one.

Brian was never an easy pupil, but we did develop a good relationship, and he became less frightened of numbers. He eventually became fairly proficient at simple addition and subtraction sums, but he never advanced much beyond that while I taught him. Still, he had made some progress and his behaviour in class improved as a consequence. I had to be happy with that.

17

From Hull And Back

As I pulled up outside Widderby Junior School one bright Spring morning, little did I realise that my working week was going to be changed yet again. Well, that was one of the good things about the job. It was never boring!

I opened the boot of the car and started to lug my bags out. I looked around to see if there was a friendly adult walking past, as my back was playing up that day, but I was out of luck. As I staggered into school, the very friendly and helpful School Secretary called out to me as I struggled past her.

I must say I found that nearly every School Secretary I came into contact with was cheerful, kind and helpful. This was despite the fact that their job had become more and more complicated and technical over the years, and their computer skills had become more developed than they could ever have dreamed when they started the job.

Their knowledge of what was going on in the school was usually second to none, and if I wanted to know anything about the school routine or future events, I always asked the Secretary rather than a teacher. The School Caretaker was often a fount of knowledge too! This particular morning I had been left a message to see the SENCo as soon as I arrived.

"Oh, heck, what have I done wrong?" I laughed, as I searched my mind for a possible reason for this request. It was a natural state of affairs for me or my colleagues to feel guilty when asked to see the Headteacher or someone else in authority in a school. This was not due to a guilty conscience, and I can't speak for others, but in my case it was due to a lack of self-confidence in my own abilities. That's why I could understand children with SEN. I could identify with them.

I knocked on the SENCo's door and waited for her to answer. She was often on the 'phone so I waited patiently. After a while I heard, "Come in!"

She looked rather stressed, well, even more stressed, this morning, surrounded by paperwork and half-drunk mugs of coffee.

"Ah, yes, Pam." She looked bewildered for a couple of seconds, then remembered why she needed to see me.

"I have a new pupil for you if you are interested."

Hmm, my timetable was really as full as I wanted it, but as I already had three pupils at this school, at least I wouldn't have to factor travelling time into my work schedule. Sometimes it could take half an hour to go from one school to another, and that time was unpaid, so obviously the nearer to each other the schools were, the better. Having many pupils in one school was better still.

"This is a bit sudden, isn't it?" I replied. There had been no mention of this the day before when I had been talking to her.

"Yes, Tony suddenly appeared in the Office this morning with his father, having moved from Hull. Family problems, I believe, and they came to York in rather a hurry."

I nodded sympathetically. This was a familiar story. "How old is he?"

"He's ten, but he looks much younger, and seems to be quite young too."

"What about the mother?"

"There's no sign of Mum yet and Dad didn't want to hang around. Basically, he just dumped Tony, then hurried off. But he did bring along a lot of paperwork from Tony's previous school, and as he already has a Statement we need to give him the extra support. Are you up for it?"

The pleading look in her eyes rang warning bells.

"So, go on, tell me, I suppose that, as usual, he has behaviour problems?"

"Tony or his Dad?" she laughed ruefully.

"Well, I did mean Tony, but ..." I tailed off. Many of the parents of the children with behaviour problems had behaviour problems of their own.

"No, I think you'll find that Tony is, in fact, very nervous, almost cowed, and I must warn you that he has a bad stammer. I don't think that you'll have any trouble from him."

Well, that was something. It would make a nice change too.

"Go on, then," I declared, "I'll take him on."

The SENCo looked relieved and passed me a rather thick file with Tony's name on it.

"Just a little light reading for you," she grimaced. "Best of luck."

After filling me in on the basic information I would need to know, I went down to the classroom to meet my newest pupil.

He was a very small boy, with a thin, pinched face under a mop of fair, straggly hair. As the teacher introduced him to me he never once lifted his eyes from the floor. She raised her eyebrows at me in a gesture which said, help!

I walked him down to my room and sat him down.

"So, Tony, I'll tell you a bit about myself, then you can tell me about yourself, and we can get to know each other. Is that OK?"

He nodded warily.

I rabbited on, telling him about my favourite food, what I liked to watch on television, what my hobbies were and so on.

"So, what do you like to watch on television, Tony?"

"N-n-n-n-nothing."

"What do you like to eat then?"

"N-n-n-n-nothing."

"Do you like to play football?" I was usually on safe ground with that one.

"N-n-n-n-no."

Oh, give me strength, I thought, although my face showed no sign of the frustration that I was feeling.

All the time I was talking, I was aware that he was trembling and this was getting worse as I questioned him. Was I really so frightening? I stopped asking him questions and got out my stickers.

"These are what I give to children when they try really hard," I told him. "It doesn't matter if the children get things wrong, as long as they try hard."

There was no reaction. Was it me, or was he like this with everyone? All the time there was no eye contact and the only thing he seemed to find interesting was the floor.

The time dragged as I tried to get a response from him, but no matter what I said, he just 'blanked' me. To be honest, I couldn't wait to take him back to his classroom, and go and get one of the other children.

At break time his teacher and I compared notes. He

hadn't been any more responsive in class and we were both coming to the conclusion that we were dealing with a traumatised child.

We found out later that Tony's Dad was a minor criminal in Hull and had got himself involved with a much more serious gang of villains. They had fled Hull in order to escape their reprisals, for what we were never sure, but it had been imperative that they got out of town. As to where Tony's Mum was we were never sure either, but if you mentioned her to Tony, his eyes filled with tears, so a hasty change of subject was necessary.

It was like treading on eggshells working with Tony, and we all had to be very careful how we spoke to him, what we said, and what we did with him.

As he had had a Statement for some time there was quite a lot of paperwork. His previous school had sent examples of his work and all the record sheets from his first SBAT Tutor.

It was obvious that he had been well taught and he was not as far behind with his work as I had at first thought. I did not want to push him too hard, though, as I didn't want to add to his problems. I wanted Tony to see my room as a haven where he could relax and possibly have a good time. Well, that was the theory anyway and it's always good to aim high!

I started him on the reading scheme I used which was aimed primarily at boys, but I began on a level that was easy for him. I had to build his confidence up and encourage him to trust me.

He soon learned the vocabulary and read the books fairly easily, although always in a nervous, faltering voice. He still couldn't look at me but it was early days yet. The most disturbing thing was his stammer, which made him difficult to understand and, of course, made him an easy target for the more thoughtless children.

In a way it was much easier working with a lively, challenging child. I was used to that situation, while with Tony I had to watch every word I said, and any sudden movement, or a knock at my door would see him flinch and cower. It was not pleasant to see, and he was often in my thoughts as I taught the other children, cooked the evening meal, lay in the bath etc. How could I break down the barriers that he had erected between himself and the cruel world?

We soon realised that Tony was a good artist, despite his reluctance to put pencil to paper when there was anybody around to watch him, or see his finished efforts.

As I dabbled in watercolour painting I was very interested in his work and how he accomplished it. I soon came to see that he couldn't bear to be watched as he drew. I, too, hated to be watched so I could sympathise!

He didn't have much confidence in his drawing and would often appear to be exasperated by it. Yep, I could identify with that, too.

Pity the poor Art Tutor who had me as a pupil!

I decided to bring in some of my own artwork to show Tony, so one morning I staggered into school even more laden down with bags and a portfolio of my artwork. That's rather a grand name for the few pictures that hadn't ended up in the bin!

I set a few out on the table and went to collect Tony. As he came into my room and he spotted the pictures, a flicker of interest registered on his face. Well, that was a good start anyway.

I started to talk about the pictures, telling him what I liked or didn't like about them, the subject matter, the problems I'd had in painting them, absolutely anything.

To my surprise, he picked one up. It was the seaside picture, one of my first efforts, which I had partly done from memory, with the aid of instructions for painting a similar picture in a book.

"I l-l-like this."

The comment, unsolicited, and said with enthusiasm, stopped me in my tracks.

I was so surprised and gratified that for a few seconds I was lost for words. Not a common occurrence! I couldn't wait to tell his teacher, the SENCo, the Headteacher, my boss, my husband, well, anybody who would listen really!

He looked up from the table and almost looked at me. "It's g-good."

That was two sentences now and I was on cloud nine! We spent the rest of that lesson talking about painting although it was still me doing most of the talking.

I couldn't wait for the morning break when I could talk to his teacher. Oh, heck, she was on duty in the playground. The day was a cold, raw November one and on days such as these, I was always grateful that SBAT Tutors didn't have to go outside on duty. Such was my desire to share my good news though, that I put on my coat and braved the cold to tell his Class Teacher about the breakthrough.

In between dealing with injuries, arguments and attempts to start World War III, just another day in a school playground then, she tried to give me her attention, and was duly thrilled and heartened by my news.

The next day when I went to collect Tony he seemed to be searching in his book bag for something. I tried not to appear impatient. I always tried to get the children out of the classroom quickly, so that I didn't disturb the lesson too much.

At last he found what he was looking for and came over to join me.

As we walked down the corridor he seemed to be plucking up the courage to say something.

"I d-d-did this l-l-last n-n-night," he said gruffly, as he thrust a piece of grubby paper under my nose.

I unfolded it and stared at the beautiful drawing of a horse.

"I c-c-copied it from a b-b-book," he said.

That didn't matter to me. In my art class we often tried to copy pictures from books. The horse had character and his body gave the impression of movement. It was very good and I told him so.

He seemed pleased but you could never tell with Tony. Was that a smile hovering on his lips? If it was, it didn't last long and his usual impassive look came back.

However, an idea was forming in my mind and I took a risk and went for it. Maybe I was hurrying things along too quickly, but life is all about taking risks so I decided to plunge in.

"When I make games for children I often need to draw pictures on them to make them look more interesting and attractive. Would you do the drawings for me, please, Tony? I don't usually have the time and it would be a real help for me."

He looked very surprised, but seemed to be pleased.

"Y-y-yeah, OK, then," he whispered.

So that was the start of a good partnership. I would make the games and write on in pencil what the illustration needed to be. Sometimes we would look in the Library for a suitable picture that he could copy. That activity improved his Library skills, so as well as helping him with his self-esteem, he was learning skills which he could use all through his life. He did the drawings at the end of our sessions, or sometimes he would knock on my door at playtime or lunch time, especially if it was raining, to see if I was there, and he could do a bit more then.

The Staff, too, were very encouraging, and Tony became known as a brilliant artist. If the children had to design posters or something similar, he really came into his own, and the other children looked to him as an expert.

Then the day came when everything went wrong. It had been a normal Thursday, well, as normal as SEN teaching days can be! At the end of the school day I was tidying my room and packing all my things away. Suddenly the door burst open and Tony's Dad stood there. Tony was cowering behind him, looking fearful and defeated.

"What the hell is all this drawing about?" he yelled at me.

How I longed for a panic button in my room so that I could get help.

"Why are you keeping him in at playtimes when he should be out playing football, not nancying around with you?"

I tried to defend myself.

"I'm not keeping him in at playtimes."

Then I saw Tony's agonised face. I didn't want to make things any worse for him, so I backed down.

"Tony is a good artist and..."

"What use is that going to be in his life, eh?" he shouted at me.

He advanced towards me and …

"I'll deal with this, Mrs Young!"

Thank goodness the cavalry had arrived in the shape of Mr Fox. Never had I been so pleased to see him! Apparently the cleaner on my corridor had heard the shouting and had gone to get help. The first person she had bumped into had been Mr Fox, and as he had been nearby he had been able to get to me quickly.

Tony's Dad seemed to shrink a little as he realised there were two of us now, and that one of us had real authority.

My main concern in all this was Tony and what this scene would be doing to him. I could see why he always appeared to be cowed and downtrodden.

"We'll go down to my office and sort this out," Mr Fox said firmly and set off, not giving him the chance to argue. Tony's Dad didn't really have any choice but to follow him, and Tony trailed disconsolately behind him.

As Mr Fox went past the next classroom, he opened the door and spoke to the teacher. I couldn't hear what he said but the next minute she was in my room, comforting me as I sat there trembling. A cup of tea, the great British panacea, miraculously appeared and she gave up her precious time to talk to me and reassure me that I hadn't done anything wrong.

I heard the words but they wouldn't go into my brain and register. My self-esteem had taken a knock and I felt like the worst SBAT Tutor in the world.

That night I hardly slept as I worried about Tony and what would happen to him. My worries were fully justified the next morning as I walked wearily into school.

"My, you look tired," said the Secretary. "Must have been a good night last night!"

I smiled wanly and moved on quickly. I was too tearful and upset and just wanted to get to the privacy of my room.

As I went to get Tony my heart was full of dread. I knew that he wouldn't be there and I was right.

I never saw him again. I never had the chance to say goodbye.

Apparently his Dad had a real row with Mr Fox as he told him what was wrong with his school and all the Staff, and that he had had enough of us and was taking Tony to a better school.

Resisting the urge to tell him that the last OFSTED report had graded his school as 'Outstanding', Mr Fox declined to argue with him, and had watched him flounce out of his school, never to be seen again.

We heard eventually that he had gone back to Hull with Tony, and a school there requested his records, so at least we knew he was in the education system. I missed him a lot.

18

Sleepless Nights!

When I started working at Tedbury Primary School, the SENCo and I had a meeting about the pupils for whom I would be responsible.

I was slightly apprehensive but was managing to keep a grip on things, when Bill bowled me a googly.

"Now, I must tell you about Martin," he said calmly. "He's in the Reception class and as well as having learning problems, which is where you come in, he has a serious medical condition, and in the worst case scenario he could die on us!"

"What?!" I was already overloaded with information and my nerve was on the point of deserting me when he said that. Could I possibly resign before I had started the job? Then I twigged. Bill was known for his wicked sense of humour.

"You're winding me up, aren't you? Ha! Ha!" I said in my best sarcastic voice.

One look at Bill's face told me that I was clutching at straws.

"No, I'm afraid I'm deadly serious, Pam. I wish I wasn't."

"Right, tell me more," I said, and prepared to wade through the paperwork which this young child had already amassed.

It was quite humbling to read about him. He had a serious case of diabetes with many complications. After a traumatic birth with forceps, he had been found to have developmental delays, and so was having learning difficulties, and he had a squint in one eye too. How could a little child have so many things wrong with him? How unfair!

"The good news is that he is a lovely little boy who behaves beautifully, and his parents are really nice," Bill declared in a cheerful voice.

"Well, that's something!" I said, trying to sound positive.

"I think the best thing for you to do first is talk to his Class Teacher, then arrange to talk to his parents," Bill said firmly.

So, that's what I did, and I soon found myself, in theory at least, equipped to deal with Martin's learning and medical problems, knowing that if he did become ill when he was with me, not only would I know what to do, but I would have back-up from the rest of the Staff, especially the Secretaries.

The main problem from our point of view seemed to be that he had hypoglycaemic episodes as a result of the diabetes where, if attention wasn't sought straight away, he could go into a coma.

Martin was too young to recognise when he was becoming poorly, so the Staff had to supervise him at all times, and if they recognised the signs they had to get something sweet into him, like a biscuit or a sugary drink. Of course, when he felt poorly he didn't want to eat or drink so that was a major hurdle. The most comforting thing was that Martin's Mum didn't work, because of her son's condition, and so was only a 'phone call away. She lived five minutes from the school and we knew that she would always come and take charge.

Bill was right, too, in that his parents were lovely and we got on well right from the start. They both had a good sense of humour, which was just as well in the situation, and they soon put me at my ease. Hang on, wasn't I supposed to be reassuring them?

The thing was that we had no experience of this situation. No amount of training could prepare you for this, and we decided to be honest with them right from the outset.

"You must tell us what we need to do," was always our mantra. They knew Martin best, what his needs were, and how best to treat him. We didn't. Sometimes professionals, in any job, are a bit precious and think that they know best, but we knew we needed guidance and we weren't afraid to admit it. There was a child's life at stake here.

As a teacher with many years' experience, and as a Specialist in SEN, some people would expect me to know what to do, but I didn't, and was more than happy to accept any advice and help.

I was also lucky in that Martin's teacher, a lovely, efficient lady called Roz who was fazed by nothing, was a joy to work with and was determined to make this situation a success.

When we appointed a lady to be Martin's 'minder' to keep an eye on him at all times, particularly playtimes and later, lunch times, we again struck lucky and found a very pleasant lady. We all worked well as a team and review meetings, which were held very frequently at first, became social occasions where much laughter could be heard.

Although I had my own room where I taught, it was right at the other end of the school from the Office, so when I took Martin I worked in a room that was almost next door to the Secretaries. They could ring Martin's Mum immediately if we felt we needed her. We tried to keep things just the same for Martin as for any other child so a little girl called Stacey came with him. They were at a similar stage, although she was slightly ahead of Martin.

Again, I was lucky in that she was a lovely girl, and I trained her to go to the Office in an emergency, with a note saying that Martin was ill and I could do with some help. The note was typed out in large black letters on a red card, so that all she had to do was enter the Office waving that and somebody would spring into action.

All the children in his class became used to seeing Martin unwell, and learned to cope with it, and to tell an adult if they saw the signs. Even very young children can behave in a very responsible manner when they have to. That is an advantage of children with SEN being included in a mainstream school. It can bring out the caring side of children, encouraging them to be helpful, and developing their sense of empathy.

I once taught in a school that had a Unit for children with partial hearing. They were integrated for as many lessons as possible into mainstream classes. I used to take a little boy from the Unit in my PE lessons and I also had a girl in my class who had behaviour problems. Gosh, she was wild! She could be very defiant and naughty, but in PE she would 'adopt' this little boy, and help him in a really caring and sympathetic way. In fact, she became a different child and it was wonderful to see.

My first meeting with Martin was a joy. He was a fair-haired small child who, not surprisingly, looked quite pale and wan. When he smiled though, which he did frequently, his whole face lit up and he positively beamed.

I went into his classroom and was introduced by Roz. "Martin, this is Mrs Young who is going to help you with your work."

"Oh, hello," beamed Martin, and then he held his hand out to shake mine! I couldn't believe it. I just wasn't used to this level of politeness!

I was almost tempted to say, "Hey, what's your game, then?" but fortunately I managed to restrain myself.

As we set off for my room he chatted away quite amiably, telling me all about how he sometimes became poorly, but he was sure I would know what to do. His faith in me was touching and I just hoped I would rise to the occasion.

The first time Martin became unwell, his teacher got a message to the Secretaries immediately, and while the Nursery Assistant tried to get him to eat and drink something, they rang his Mum, hoping desperately that she would be there. What if she was shopping? She had to go out sometime. Fortunately she was there and she appeared at school in a few minutes. Gosh, she was fit, that woman! She must have run and she was hardly out of breath!

She sorted Martin out, then turned to the members of Staff, including me, who were all hovering, trying to look useful but failing miserably.

"Are you OK?" She looked solicitously at us. As one, our knees gave way and in sheer relief we sank into chairs. As long as the emergency was on we were prepared and ready, but as soon as things were alright again we went to jelly. But we became more and more accustomed to seeing Martin unwell, and our well-rehearsed plans swung into action almost automatically.

As Martin became older he often had to go into hospital for tests and treatment, but his attendance at school was otherwise very good. He would sometimes be a bit off colour, but he always wanted to come to school and we respected his attitude. He wanted to be like the other children - what young child doesn't?

Getting the balance right between coping with his medical needs and not treating him any differently was hard, but I think we did the best we could.

The day came, though, when Martin's Mum wanted to go out a bit more and who could blame her? Martin was getting much better and could recognise when he was feeling off colour. Mum would always be on the end of a 'phone (thank goodness for mobile 'phones), but sometimes she wouldn't be able to get to us as quickly as before.

Resisting the urge to panic when she told us this, we listened carefully to the contingency plan - to get an ambulance. Apparently we had half an hour to get Martin to hospital, where he was well known, before the situation became very serious. We would also have to explain when we made the 999 call exactly what the problem was, so the medical staff could take action very quickly when they got to Martin.

We never did have to call an ambulance, although every member of Staff was trained to do just that if needed. They were a fantastic lot, particularly the School Secretaries, who were always so supportive and willing to help.

One day Martin's Mum came to Bill, the SENCo,

and requested a meeting. Expecting to be told that there had been a change in Martin's condition, or that there was a new problem with his schooling, we were totally unprepared for the news that we heard.

"We're moving house." Martin's Mum looked pleased and nervous both at the same time.

I gaped at her. "But why? Aren't you happy with us?" She sought to reassure me.

"We are very happy with the way you have all treated Martin and we know how lucky we are, but we need to be nearer my parents, especially as I've got a part-time job. They could help us much more and take some of the strain from us."

I could see that, but…

"The job is at Straffham," she named a small town twenty miles away, "and my parents live there as well. The house we've found has a bigger garden and it's just lovely. It's in the country and we've always wanted to live there."

"What about a hospital, though?" I queried.

"Yes, there's a small but efficient hospital, and they assure me that they can deal with Martin. We'll come back to York and Leeds for Specialist appointments but that will be fine."

I felt an unexplained sense of loss. I had thought that Martin would be with us until he went to Secondary School and we had invested so much time and effort in him. Would another school be able to cope? Don't be so arrogant, I thought. If we had learnt to cope, then another school could, of course.

"There's just one thing," Martin's Mum said, bringing me back to reality. "Would you all come with me to his new school and talk to the Headteacher and

Staff about him?"

"Of course we will," we replied, and we fixed a time that would be suitable for us all.

I say for us all because we decided that all the Staff involved in Martin's care would go on this visit, so one day, after school, four of us set off for Straffham in Bill's car.

I don't know why but I felt very apprehensive and uneasy, and as we drove along I mentioned my fears to the others.

"That's odd!" said Roz. "That's the way I feel too, although I couldn't say why."

The other two agreed that they weren't really looking forward to the visit, but we all said we would be very upbeat and positive when we got there.

None of us knew the school where we were heading but, following instructions from Martin's Mum, we pulled up outside with minutes to spare.

We announced who we were to the Secretary and were asked to wait. Martin's Mum and Dad appeared at that moment, having been stuck behind a combine harvester for most of their journey. They were understandably feeling a bit flustered as they were afraid they were going to be late, and I could see that Mum was a bit on edge and tearful.

So, we waited and we waited until, after fifteen minutes, I decided to see what the delay was. As I approached the Secretary again, a door opened and the Headteacher came out. About time, I thought, but hopefully managing to keep my feelings to myself, I stretched out my hand and introduced myself.

He seemed to be very friendly, and he took us down to Martin's new classroom where the meeting was to take place. There, waiting for us, were all three Class Teachers and two Teaching Assistants.

Now, I'm very susceptible to atmospheres and I sensed immediately their hostility towards us. I glanced at my colleagues and very slightly raised my eyebrows. They told me later that they had all felt the same, but obviously we couldn't say anything.

I just daren't look at Martin's parents. I knew them very well by this time and I had a horrible feeling that I knew what they were thinking as well.

We explained how we catered for Martin's needs and emphasised that, although his condition was serious and he needed a lot of attention, it wasn't as difficult as it looked on paper.

We were all very surprised when one of the teachers blurted out, "Well, I don't see how we could possibly cope with him, given our resources!"

Bill looked her in the eye. "But you would have the same resources we've got. It's not a problem once you've got used to it."

One of the others chimed in, "It's too much of a responsibility for us. We couldn't watch him all the time!"

I couldn't believe my ears! So it was OK for us to take on this, admittedly huge, responsibility but it wasn't for them!

I looked at the Headteacher, who seemed to be a bit ineffective. He blustered a bit but whatever we said the Staff would come back at us with very negative comments. They had obviously been discussing this ever since we made the appointment, and their minds had been made up before we had arrived. Of course, legally they couldn't refuse to accept Martin but who would want to work with such negativity?

As we walked out to the car, having left everything up in the air, we were stunned. Martin's Mum looked distraught and I said I would ring her tomorrow, when we'd had a chance to reflect on the situation.

As we drove off in silence, I broke it by saying, "I don't think that Martin's Mum will get any sleep tonight!"

That led to a torrent of angry remarks about what we had just experienced.

"How could they be so awful!"

"Why won't they give him a chance?"

"I couldn't believe their attitude!"

"I'm not happy about Martin going there!"

I didn't get much sleep myself that night.

At half past eight the next morning Bill received a 'phone call from Martin's Mum.

"Can I come and see you straight away, please?"

"Of course you can," Bill reassured her. "Come to my room as soon as you've dropped Martin off."

He wondered what she was going to say and hurried off to find Roz, and then me, to tell us that Martin's Mum wanted to see him.

"Let me know what she says, won't you," we both urged him.

Just after nine o'clock, Martin's Mum knocked and put her head round my door.

"Can I come in? I've just been to see Bill and I thought I'd come and have a word with you."

I was just about to go and get my next pupil but I decided that Martin's Mum needed me more. I could take the pupil later.

She looked dreadful and, knowing her as well as I

did, I couldn't stop myself from saying, "You didn't sleep much last night, did you?"

She grimaced. "Is it that obvious?"

I laughed. "Well, to be truthful, you do look a bit tired."

"Yes, well, I was so angry and upset about yesterday. To be fair, I think that the Headteacher was open to the idea of having Martin at his school, but he was on his own. The rest of the Staff were so hostile, weren't they?"

"Yes, I can only agree with you there."

I waited.

"So, we've come to a decision, Pam. There's no way we can send Martin to that school. The move is off. We've always known how good you've all been here but we appreciate you even more after yesterday. Possibly we've been a bit spoiled, but their attitude was so bad that we want Martin to stay here with all of you."

I stared at her.

"But what about your job, being near to your parents, the new house and the big garden?"

"They don't matter if Martin won't be happy. Anyway, I've already rung the Headteacher and told him about our decision. He couldn't keep the relief out of his voice," she ended up bitterly.

And then the tears came and I reached out for my ever-ready box of tissues. I think it was a release for her, and she knew that my room was a safe haven where she could cry. I needed a few tissues myself as I couldn't bear the thought of Martin at that school. "There will be other jobs and we've decided to get an allotment."

Sleepless Nights!

We suddenly both burst out laughing at the thought that an allotment would solve their problems!

"It'll make up for the garden," she tried to explain, laughing between her tears.

"I know," I laughed as well. "I'm just laughing out of sheer relief that you're not going!"

Half an hour later I tiptoed into Martin's classroom. I went up to Roz and whispered, "They're not going!" She punched her fist into the air. "I know, Bill's already been to see me!"

I grinned.

"Couldn't you bear the thought of him going to that school either?"

"No, definitely not. And I'll tell you something else. I didn't sleep very well last night!"

When Martin's 'minder' appeared she was also told the good news.

"Oh, thank goodness! I didn't sleep much last night for worrying about him!"

Well, what a lot of worriers we were! And I was very proud of us all for being so!

The next day I made a point of seeing Martin's Mum in the playground before school.

"How did you sleep last night?" I asked, smiling.

"Like a log!" she grinned. "How about you?"

"Like a log!" I grinned back.

Now that's what I call a happy ending!

Martin stayed with us until he was eleven years old and then it was time for him to transfer to the local Comprehensive School.

His health had improved, although he still needed much attention and care, but he had become more responsible about looking after himself.

Bill arranged a meeting with Martin's parents and the SENCo at his new school. She couldn't have been nicer and she was so receptive to everything that was said. The meeting was totally different to the other one, and they both came out smiling and reassured.

It was a wrench to see Martin go, but it had to happen and we all knew that he was going to the right school. He did really well and with all the extra tuition he had right through his schooling he caught up with many of his peers. He even got six GCSEs five years later! Result!

19

"You'll like Charlie!"

I have emphasised throughout this book how almost all of the children I taught had low self-esteem, or, indeed, no self-esteem.

Well, there is always the exception that proves the rule, and that exception was Charlie.

Charlie was a pupil at St. Crispin's School, a modern newly constructed school, six miles out of the city. I nearly didn't take him on because, being quite a long way out of town, it took half an hour to get there, and I didn't get paid for my travelling time, although I could claim expenses.

If I got behind a slow-moving vehicle, like a tractor, on the narrow, country roads then I would feel under pressure as the clock ticked on, and I would arrive feeling stressed and in need of a pick me up!

My boss knew how to press the right buttons, though.

"You'll like Charlie," she assured me. "He's a bit of a character!"

"Has he got behaviour problems?" I asked, as I was feeling a bit worn down by pupils who were 'challenging'.

"Not really," came the slightly less than reassuring answer, and she laughed. "He's very cheerful and exuberant, but he's not defiant or naughty. Honestly, you'll like him."

Methinks she does protest too much, I thought but…

"Oh, go on, then," I acquiesced. "I'll take him on."

So, one wet Wednesday afternoon, I duly presented myself at his classroom, where a very pleasant young teacher acknowledged who I was and called out, "Charlie, could you come here, please?"

I was used to teachers being a bit more subtle and discreet than that, but I soon learned that you didn't have to worry about that with Charlie. He didn't do subtle or discreet.

I can only describe him as being like Tigger in the Winnie the Pooh stories, as he bounced over to us with a huge, infectious grin on his face.

He was a small boy with a shock of ginger hair and the freckles to go with it. The other children called him Carrot Top and he didn't mind one bit. Charlie didn't mind much really. He was only six years old so he was my youngest pupil, and he still had the eagerness and enthusiasm that most Infant children have.

"This is Mrs Young who has come to help you," the teacher introduced me. "Now look after her, won't you, as she doesn't know our school and might get lost."

What's this 'might'? I thought as Charlie ushered me out of the classroom and down the corridor to the room that had been earmarked for us. He bounced along beside me, eager to chat and find out about me. I wasn't used to this friendliness and concern!

"Isn't it a wet day? We couldn't go out at lunch time so I played Snakes and Ladders with my friends. That was good fun. Have you come in a car? What sort is it? What are we going to do? Is that bag heavy? I'll carry it for you. Here we are!"

Thank goodness it hadn't been far, because I was wilting already under this interrogation. He opened the door and then stepped back to let me go in first. I was tempted to ask what his game was as I wasn't used to such chivalry, but I just smiled and mumbled my thanks.

He was so cheerful! I just wasn't used to this at all and at first I wasn't too sure what to make of him. Could I stand all this jollity?

I asked him to sit down at the desk and he did so - for one minute any way.

"Cor, look at that rain!" he exclaimed, bouncing across to the window.

"Charlie, could you come back here, please," I asked, fearing that I had already lost his attention.

"Oh, sorry, Miss Young!" he cried and immediately shot back into his seat.

I wasn't used to immediate obedience either so that rattled me!

He didn't actually sit properly but, one step at a time, I thought, and I started to talk to him about what he liked best at school.

"Everything!"

What did he like to watch on television?

"Everything for children!"

Was there anything that he didn't like at school?

"No, I like everything!"

What did he like to eat?

Yes, you've guessed.

"Everything, really!"

Charlie was so positive and cheerful about everything, so I risked asking him if he was good at reading and writing.

"Oh, yes, I'm good at most things really!"

This reply didn't quite tally with the reports I had read about his learning difficulties, which were quite severe.

A child didn't get a Statement at the age of six years

old without being in considerable difficulties. Charlie had Dyspraxia, also known as the 'clumsy child' syndrome, and his inability to learn even the basic skills of Literacy had pointed us in the direction of Dyslexia, although at his young age it was difficult to give a firm diagnosis.

It was very interesting that Charlie didn't see that he had any problems.

As I started to do my own assessments of Charlie in the following weeks, he amazed me by the absolute certainty with which he approached the tasks I gave him to do. Take his spelling, for a start.

I always had to introduce the spelling tests in a very sensitive and fun way, knowing that at any minute the child would throw his pencil down and refuse to go any further.

"I can't do that!" would be a familiar refrain.

Charlie didn't know the meaning of the word 'can't'.

"I wonder if you could just have a go at writing a few words for me, Charlie?"

He smiled eagerly at me and nodded his head.

"They might be a bit hard, so if you can't do it just tell me and we'll stop."

"No, that will be OK, Miss Young," he reassured me. He was reassuring me!

He found it very difficult to write, even to hold a pencil, because of his Dyspraxia, and his ability to form his letters was very poor.

We started off with easy words, like 'a' and 'at', 'is' and 'in'.

"Oh yes, I can do that!" he would say after every word that I gave him, and we soon got onto much harder words.

Hmm, this was interesting, and I couldn't wait to mark his work later when he had gone.

The page of squiggles and haphazard marks would have made a drunken spider with a fountain pen proud.

I couldn't make out one word, and yet, he had been so sure that he could spell them all.

This was always a bone of contention between us, but eventually, with a great deal of hard work, his writing improved drastically, although we did have a few friendly battles on the way, as he sometimes thought that he knew better than me. He was always trying to show me the error of my ways! But, my attempts to persuade him that he didn't always know the correct way to spell a word fell on deaf ears.

I always taught the children to try a word they weren't sure about on a 'try pad', so that they could see if it looked right and I could correct it if it wasn't. But Charlie only did this reluctantly and, I think, in order to please me, as hey, he knew how to spell anything. If the rest of the world didn't do it his way, well, that wasn't his problem.

His teacher was equally frustrated by this, and we often got together to sympathise with each other and to compare notes on this very remarkable boy. I suppose it was a mini support group!

Charlie slowly, but surely, learned all the letters of the alphabet, their sounds and how to write them. He was also learning to word build simple three letter, regular words, like 'cat' and 'dog'.

I decided that I would start him on a reading scheme I had used with most of the boys, and with which I had great success on a regular basis. I took the first book out of my bag and showed it to him.

Charlie was over the moon! "Oh, Miss Young, that's fantastic! I can't wait to show my teacher, and Matt and Ben."

He had named his two close friends. The three of them were inseparable, and Matt and Ben were there to defend Charlie if any misguided child tried to tease him about his ginger hair or his Special Needs. There weren't many who tried though, probably because of his engaging personality and friendliness.

He went back to his classroom on cloud nine that day and, I must say, that his enthusiasm was infectious. I floated out of the school with a big grin on my face, and the memory of the child in a previous school who had called me a 'cow' evaporated.

Ah, the ups and downs of being an SBAT Tutor!

One day, though, Charlie's positive outlook on life was very misplaced. I fetched him from his class-room straight after playtime.

As he bounced down the corridor he repeatedly told me about the goal he had just saved in the play ground. His Dyspraxia meant that running about, particularly controlling the ball, was too difficult for him, but his friends soon came up with the solution and he became the goalie.

Realising that he would find this task rather difficult, they made sure they were brilliant in defence, and Charlie wasn't usually troubled too much. If he did let a goal in, well, it wasn't the end of the world, and their friendship overcame everything. This was a pretty unusual relationship in children so young, and it was a really pleasant and unexpected surprise to us all.

This particular playtime, the defence had let the ball get past them, and their cries of, "Charlie, look out! Save it!" had woken Charlie up from his thoughts about what he was having for lunch. For once he dived the right way and by sheer fluke he saved the goal!

He had been mobbed by his rather surprised team mates, and only the bell for the end of playtime had stopped their rowdy celebrations. I had one very excited little boy to deal with!

As he bounced into the room and sat down I noticed that he winced as he put his arms on the table. I was immediately on the alert.

"Have you hurt your arm, Charlie?" I asked.

"Nah, only a bit, Miss Young. I think when I dived across the goal - you should have seen it, it was brilliant! You see, Matt shouted to me that the ball was coming and..."

He was off again, reliving the moment, but then he suddenly tailed off as he moved his arms to show me how he had become a hero. As he did so, some of the colour drained from his face.

"Did you tell the teacher in the playground that you'd hurt your arm?"

"No way! I was too busy being David Beckham!"

"Let me have a look, Charlie," I said firmly.

"It's alright, Miss Young, it only hurts a bit."

After a bit of persuasion, he turned back his shirt sleeve. His arm was swollen and the bruising was already starting to come out. My teacher's sixth sense kicked in and I suspected that it was broken. I took him back to his teacher and showed her his arm. She acknowledged my fears and I took him down to the Secretary to ask her to ring his Mum up and get him to hospital. I hoped desperately that she would be in, as things could become complicated if parents can't be contacted in a situation like this.

Fortunately, she was at home, and, as she lived very close to school, she was there in an instant. However, she didn't have a car. The answer was simple and Charlie, who was by now very quiet, a worrying thing in itself, and his Mum, were soon in my car on the way to York Hospital.

His arm was indeed broken, although it was a clean break, and there were no complications to worry about. He insisted on returning to school after a few days, and was greeted as a conquering hero by his classmates.

Matt and Ben rose to the occasion and whatever Charlie couldn't manage to do for himself, they rushed to his side to help. The whole experience just confirmed to me that Charlie was, indeed, a very special child.

Sports Day was also a day when you would think that Charlie would be a bit down-hearted. Most school Sports Days consist of two elements; the 'potted' sports, where all the children moved round activities that every child could have a go at, and the running races.

For a child with Dyspraxia, running wasn't that easy, and I wondered how Charlie would feel about the races.

"It'll be good, Miss Young! I can't wait for Sports Day!" he enthused.

Was there no end to this child's jollity?

"Are you running in one of the races?" I queried, just

making sure that he was competing with the other children.

"Oh, yes," he said. "I've been practising with Ben and Matt."

Those boys deserved a medal for all their devotion to Charlie. I checked later with Charlie's teacher and she confirmed that, indeed, Charlie was running in the races.

"I wouldn't dare suggest that he didn't!" she said, shrugging her shoulders.

I made the effort to come and support Charlie on Sports Day and, as he lined up with five other boys in his race, the butterflies were fluttering round my tummy.

I found his class and their teacher and settled down to watch his race. He looked so cheerful and when he came in last, although not by much, with his arms raised and a triumphant smile on his face, it seemed as if the whole school roared their approval. They knew how much effort it had taken for him not to trip up and to complete the course. I turned to his teacher and, with a smile she passed me the box of tissues - she had come well prepared and we both dabbed at our eyes together!

§

Every child who had a Statement had to have an Annual Review. All the adults involved in the child's education and care were asked to attend, so there could be a very formidable array of Professionals at the meeting. I know that many parents and teachers found them a bit overwhelming, so I was rather bemused when it was decided that the children should also attend, although common sense prevailed and they were only brought in for the final few minutes. Their opinion was sought on their progress and a mumbled, "Alright" was all we could hope for from most of them.

It was always my job to go and get the child from their classroom, and having already briefed them in their lessons with me about what would happen, and the kind of thing they could say, I would again witter on, trying to reassure them. They were always so nervous, and I always insisted that if a child didn't want to come they didn't have to put themselves through the ordeal.

Most children agreed to attend which I thought said a lot about them. If I'd had the choice I would often have preferred not to bother!

My stock answer when a child confessed to me on the way to the meeting that they didn't know what to say was always, "Well, you could always say what a brilliant teacher I am, and that I need a pay rise!"

The children, all used to my sense of humour, would smile wanly and then forget it.

Charlie, as you can imagine, had no qualms about attending the meeting, and he skipped happily along beside me, asking me who was there, what had been said, and did I think that it would be burgers for lunch. Eh? Run that last one past me again, will you? I had made my usual comment about my teaching ability and about needing a pay rise and then forgot all about it.

As we entered the room, Charlie beamed at everybody and, looking at each person in turn, said

"Hello!" to every single person. There were eight of us in total!

The Headteacher smiled and said, "Would you like to sit down Charlie, and tell us how you think you are doing. Everybody here agrees that you try very hard and that you are getting much better at your work."

Charlie beamed again.

"Yes, I think that I am good at my work, and I would like to say that Miss Young is a brilliant teacher and deserves a pay rise!"

Oh no! Charlie, you weren't supposed to say that! It was a joke!

The adults all roared with laughter, while I went bright red and wished that the earth would open up and swallow me!

The Educational Psychologist, a good friend of mine who I had known for many years, couldn't resist it.

"Mrs Young, you really must stop using the children in this way! We know you're doing a good job but getting the children to plead for more money for you, well..!"

The laughter started up again and Charlie sat there, bathed in all this bonhomie, relishing every minute. Oh, Charlie, I thought, there's never a dull moment when you're around!

§

It's interesting to wonder why Charlie had such excellent self-esteem, and why other children had very little.

I think that the home background had a lot to do with it, and certainly Charlie's parents were very loving and supportive towards him. They did a lot with him out of school and he was always going somewhere or trying some new activity. They gave him time and attention and love, and they couldn't have done more than that.

If only all children were as lucky as Charlie.

20

Honesty Is The Best Policy

Regardless of their particular needs, I had always taken the approach that honesty was the best policy with the children, but it was not always easy. You may recall that I talked earlier about an occasion when a child wanted to disclose something he wanted kept secret, and I had to tell him this was not possible. Another rule was to allow the children to talk about anything which troubled them. Whenever I hear about 9/11 in the media or some other devastating terrorist attack, I think of Micky. He often gave the impression of being a tough guy, but in the days after the attacks on America he was terrified. We had one session where he kept firing questions at me.

"We're all going to die, aren't we, Miss Young?"

"They're going to bomb us next, aren't they?"

"There's going to be a war, isn't there?"

I felt so angry that these terrorists could make one of my children feel like this. On one occasion, an aeroplane flew over school and Micky was almost under the table, shaking with fear.

I had always tried to answer children truthfully and honestly, even though the answer was sometimes not what they wanted to hear. I tried to explain to him that nobody knew what was going to happen. Having lived through the Cuban Missile Crisis as a child, when the whole world held its breath, fearing we were on the brink of extinction, and many other crises had come and gone, I felt confident we would all survive this latest crisis. The world might be a more dangerous place but for Micky, at least, nothing much would change.

But mostly, I had to tell Micky that I didn't know what was going to happen. I think children often know when they are being lied to by adults, and that leads to a lack of respect, so any relationship, whether in school or out of school, must be based on trust and the truth. At the moment of writing this I've been proved right, thank goodness!

§

One day, on the way to school, Micky's companion, another Year Six boy, suggested that they go into a 'phone box and dial 999. They would ask for an ambulance but then I think their plan became a little hazy.

Unfortunately, a 'phone box was on their route, so in they went and, of course the other boy persuaded Micky to dial the number. When the operator asked which service they required he kept his head and replied, "Ambulance."

When she asked for the address Micky was thrown. His accomplice had heard what the operator had said and, being rather quicker, had told Micky to say, "Number 2, Wellington Square."

I don't know if the operator could hear the stifled giggles, but I'm sure there were some, because that was an address from a reading scheme used by me and by many other SBAT Tutors. However, the Operator was obviously not to know that and the call was taken seriously at first.

Eventually the 'phone call was treated as a hoax and traced to this particular 'phone box at that particular time. The boys were easy to trace and soon they found themselves in the Headteacher's room, being given a very stern telling off.

When I questioned Micky later he could not believe the fuss.

"But when I said Wellington Square I thought she would know that it was a joke." He looked very crestfallen.

"But Micky," I explained in as patient a manner as I could muster, though I wasn't feeling very patient, "not everybody has read the Wellington Square books and so not everybody knows that address. To her it wasn't a joke."

Micky stared at me with a look of incredulity, and said, "Everybody's heard of Wellington Square!"

Oh, give me strength, I thought, I'm not getting through to him at all. I sent him back to his class and sat and thought. To me there was only one thing to do, and that was to involve the Police, so that the boys would be aware of the gravity of the situation. At break time I sought out Bill, his Class Teacher, and suggested that I ring the local Police Station, explain the situation, and ask for their advice. Bill agreed and I duly rang up.

The very nice policeman stifled his laughter as I explained what the boys had done, and said he would ask the Community Policeman to give me a ring.

The upshot was that a very friendly, but imposing, policeman arrived at school and talked to the Year Six children about the dangers and implications of making a hoax 999 call.

We had decided not to single out Micky and his friend, but their red faces rather gave the game away. Next time I saw him he looked very chastened.

"I didn't realise what it would mean. It was stupid."
Well, he had learnt the hard way but it seemed that
he **had** learnt a lesson, and that was the important
thing. He got up to go back to his classroom.
"Oh, and Micky?"
He turned and looked warily at me.
"Yeah?"
"Find a friend you can trust - not one who will make
you do something that will get you into trouble!"
He looked very sheepish and went out muttering to
himself.
I didn't have much hope that he would take any
notice of my advice, in fact, to be honest, I had no
hope at all, but I had to say it.

§

Being honest with the children wasn't always easy,
but I always did my best. A big test came once when
I was teaching some eleven year olds in my room.
There was a door that led outside and during the
lesson I suddenly spotted the largest spider I had ever
seen on the wall inside, by the window.
I'm not keen on spiders at the best of times but this
one... well, the word tarantula came to mind, though
that might have been a bit of an exaggeration.
The three girls in the group did the really girly thing
and started shrieking at the tops of their voices.
"Aaaaargh, Mrs Young, get rid of it!"
"Oh no, it's going to get me!"
"Save me, somebody, I hate spiders!"
Yeah, you and me both, I thought, but I didn't want
the children to see my fear.

The boys, of course, were revelling in the girls' distress and were encouraging the spider to come nearer and really frighten them!

"It's OK girls." I tried to reassure them, although I wasn't managing to reassure myself.

"It won't hurt us and there's really no need to be frightened."

"Aren't you scared, Mrs Young?" asked Kenny, a large boy with a rather surly manner, but with whom I had a good relationship.

"Well, Kenny," I blustered, "they're not my all-time favourite creatures, but I wouldn't exactly say that I was scared."

No, just terrified was more the word that came to mind, but I was determined not to let him see this.

I needed to get the spider outside, without showing any fear and without killing it.

I calmly, well, as calmly as I could, got a piece of cardboard and a glass and managed to capture it.

"Right, Kenny," I said quickly, "you open the door and I'll dash out and let the spider go, and then shut the door quickly when I've finished."

He looked gleefully at me.

"I've got to shut the door quickly, Mrs Young?"

"Yes," I said impatiently. "Shut the door to stop it coming back in again."

The girls were becoming unbearable by this time so I nodded to Kenny, he opened the door, I rushed out, let the spider go, and then turned to leap back in again. I was horrified to see that the door, which was self-locking, was shut, and Kenny was standing there with a fiendish grin on his face.

"Kenny," I shouted. "Open this door at once! You

know fine well that I'm supposed to be on the inside!"
"But Mrs Young, I was only doing what you said,"
he smiled at me, when he at last opened the door and
let me in.

I had to see the funny side and we all had a good
laugh about it, but I was glad that the Headteacher
hadn't found me in dereliction of my duty by being
out of the room!

21

I Do Like A Happy Ending!

The rain was pouring down as my good friend Jane and I sat in front of the fire in her cosy little house, warming our hands on hot mugs of tea. Jane was also an SBAT Tutor and we often met up to have a good natter, swap ideas and, generally to support each other, although I often thought that she was doing more of the supporting!

This particular day I had called in to collect some books and to share thoughts on a training day that we had been to the day before.

Our talk moved on to more general aspects of our job, particularly the advantages, which were many. I couldn't resist listing all the disadvantages of being a Classroom Teacher, as we had both been previously, with all the pressures of the National Curriculum, testing etc.

Jane looked at me, and with a huge grin on her face declared, "You know, I think that we probably have the best job in education. Aren't we lucky!"

I smiled back at her, a sudden wave of euphoria flowing over me. "I think you're right, Jane."

§

I was going to end the book on that note, but during the course of writing this book, I tried to track down some of my former pupils and colleagues. I wanted to check that they approved of being in my book, if indeed they recognised themselves, as names and descriptions have been changed to protect the innocent!

I had Sam's address from when I taught him, and in some trepidation, I decided to call at his house to see if I could find him. After all, he must be about twenty one years old by now, so it was nearly ten years since I had seen him. How would he feel about meeting me again? Would he have moved house and would I be faced with strangers who wouldn't have a clue what I was talking about?

I needn't have worried. As soon as Sam opened the door I recognised him immediately.

"Hello, Sam, I don't know if you remember me, but I'm Mrs Young. I taught you at Milderton School." I braced myself for his reaction.

"Oh, yeah, hi, Mrs Young," he replied, with a big grin. "How are you?"

I smiled with relief, and realised that Sam had lost none of his social skills.

"I'm very well, thank you, Sam. How are you, and your parents?"

He told me that everybody was well, and that he had a job that he enjoyed doing, and I was very thankful for that.

I took a deep breath and prepared to tell him the reason for my visit.

"Actually, Sam, I've written a book and you're in it!"

He stepped back in surprise. "Am I? How come?"

As I explained all about the book, I waited for his response in fear and trepidation.

"Cor, that's ace, Mrs Young! I can't believe that I'm going to be in a book. That's wicked!"

I was so relieved at his reaction that I could have hugged him, but I managed to resist. That would really have been a step too far! After more chatting about old times, I left the relevant chapter with him and he promised to read it, and to show it to his parents. I arranged that I would ring him up a few days later to get his reaction.

Those three days seemed to drag by as I convinced myself that if Sam didn't hate it, his parents probably would, in fact Sam would as well, so that I would have to miss that chapter out, and that was one of the reasons for writing the book, and I wished that I'd never started the thing, and oh hell, I didn't think that I even dared to ring him up! Thank goodness, my husband reassured me that everything would be fine, and thankfully he was right.

When I did eventually ring Sam, he was very positive. "It's great, Mrs Young," he declared. "I was really chuffed with it. I don't want you to change anything." I was so relieved that I could have cried.

"There's just one thing. When the book comes out will you let me know so that I can buy a copy?"

"Sam, not only that, but I want you to come to the book launch as one of the guests of honour. Would you do that?" The smile on my face went from ear to ear.

"Yeah, I'd love to! I can't wait! When is it again?"

I put the 'phone down and went to find my husband. "There you are, then," he smiled at me. "What did I tell you? And if Sam loves the book I'm sure that the others will as well."

Well, I didn't know if I would go that far, but Sam had boosted my confidence and I picked up the 'phone again, ready to ring my next family.

As I had known Peter's family pretty well, I had no qualms in ringing them up to ask them to read the chapter about him, and to see what they would like me to change, as I hadn't pulled any punches. This they agreed to do, so I posted off the relevant piece and waited a few days.

The doubts then set in and I felt sure that they would hate it and would want me to change every word. In fact, they would probably forbid me from writing anything about him at all.

I needn't have worried as, when I plucked up the courage to ring, they said that they loved it and couldn't wait for the book to come out. I was so surprised that I could hardly stammer out my thanks.

"Actually, we wondered if you would do something for us," said Peter's Mum.

"Anything," I declared rather foolishly, still so pleased with their reaction.

"Well, it's Peter's School Presentation later this month. It's his last one as he has left school now, but he's getting two prizes and we wondered if you would like to come with us to see him receive them."

Would I? Just try stopping me! I put the 'phone down totally elated and went to tell my husband. Apparently I had another grin from ear to ear!

As I stood nervously waiting in the school entrance hall to meet Peter and his family on the evening of the Presentation, I wondered if I would recognise him and what he would think to meeting me again. After so many years would he have forgotten about our times together?

I swallowed nervously as they came through the door. Peter came towards me, hand outstretched, and as his Mum said, "You remember Mrs Young, don't you?" he looked me in the eye, shook my hand and said, "Hello, Mrs Young, how are you?"

Bearing in mind the problems that he had, this was a huge step forward in terms of his social awareness skills.

That was just the start of a wonderful evening. Peter actually went up to collect two certificates and two prizes. He had been awarded eight Grade Bs in his GCSEs which was a fantastic result, and one that the Headteacher mentioned especially in his speech. I was very impressed with the way that the achievements of the SEN children were celebrated by the school, and I was thrilled to see that yet another of my ex-pupils was also receiving a prize. As our lovely god-daughter also received many awards I spent the entire evening trying not to burst with pride! Peter was a bit embarrassed but nevertheless, he collected his prizes and responded appropriately to the guest who was giving them out. I was amused to see that the books that he had chosen were all about trains! He grinned at me as he saw me looking at them.

"I'm still interested in trains, just like I was when I was with you."

At the end of the evening I asked Peter if he could introduce me to the SENCo who had done such a wonderful job with him.

He scanned the room, then said, "Ah yes, she's over there."

He then put his hand on my arm to steer me in the right direction and guided me over. Now, from reading this book you will realise that Peter would never have done that before. In fact he would have shrunk from any physical contact. That just confirmed, if further confirmation were needed, that I needn't worry about Peter coping in the big wide world. Sure, life wouldn't always be plain sailing, but he had grown into a very pleasant young man and I enjoyed his company very much. And, with such a lovely family around him, who treated me like royalty that evening, he will get the support that he needs. What a success story! I think that I <u>will</u> finish there!